Bariatric Meal Prep
made easy

Six Weeks of Portion-Controlled Recipes to Keep the Weight Off

Kristin Willard

Registered Dietitian and
Creator of Bariatric Meal Prep

PAGE STREET
PUBLISHING CO.

PAGE STREET
PUBLISHING CO.

First published in 2022 by
Page Street Publishing Co.
27 Congress Street, Suite 1511
Salem, MA 01970
www.pagestreetpublishing.com

Distributed by Macmillan, sales in Canada by The Canadian Manda Group.

26   25   24   23   22   2   3   4   5

ISBN-13: 978-1-64567-496-2
ISBN-10: 1-64567-496-7

Library of Congress Control Number: 2021939501

Cover and book design by Molly Kate Young for Page Street Publishing Co.
Photography by Becky Winkler

Printed and bound in the United States of America

dedication

This cookbook is dedicated to the weight-loss surgery community who continue to inspire me every day.

contents

main entrées 65

introduction

What does 60 grams of protein look like?

As a bariatric dietitian, I have heard this question a million times. Sixty grams of protein is the minimum amount required to eat in a day after undergoing weight-loss surgery as set forth by the American Society for Metabolic and Bariatric Surgery (ASMBS). While it is easy to say, "Eat 60 grams of protein a day," it is much harder to put into practice because of the limited stomach size.

To help people learn how to eat properly after weight-loss surgery, I created Bariatric Meal Prep on Instagram to provide "snapshots" of what a typical day of food should look like after surgery. These pictures were very popular on social media and left people asking for more. I quickly began providing recipes and nutrition tips to help support people's journeys after undergoing bariatric surgery. After many requests for a cookbook, I am thrilled to finally be delivering this to you.

If you are reading this book, you are likely preparing for bariatric surgery or have already had it. You might be losing weight or maintaining the weight you lost. Wherever you are on your journey, you will find recipes in this cookbook to support you. I even take it one step further and show you how you can begin meal prepping as a habit to support your goals. There are shopping lists and a meal prep schedule for different diet stages as an extra level of support.

My recipes utilize whole, minimally processed foods to support your recovery and maintenance phase after surgery. I believe in the power of whole foods as a strategy for long-term success. In this cookbook, I will show you how nourishing, minimally processed foods can be easy to prepare and taste delicious. You may enjoy my Easy Parmesan Crisps (page 141) for a quick snack or my Enchilada-Stuffed Bell Peppers (page 70) for a fast weeknight meal.

Learning how to nourish your body after weight-loss surgery is about so much more than just weight loss. It is a practice of self-care that can improve your relationship with food and empower you to believe, "Yes, I can do this!" I am honored to be your guide.

Kristin Willard

the bariatric plate method

As you go through the recipes in this cookbook, you'll notice most of them follow the Bariatric Plate Method (BPM). The BPM was developed within the bariatric community to provide guidance on what your plate should consist of after bariatric surgery. The goal of the BPM is to make cooking less complicated and to teach a balanced way of eating, so you don't feel like you are depriving yourself and can enjoy food from all the food groups. When the BPM is followed consistently, weight regain is less likely to occur.

The BPM is a modern variation of the Plate Method used by the United States Department of Agriculture (USDA) to guide proper portion sizes after weight-loss surgery. It suggests 50 percent of your plate needs to be protein, 30 percent non-starchy vegetables and 20 percent carbohydrates. Now keep in mind that although this is a good general guideline to go by, not every meal has to be perfect to reap the benefits. There is some flexibility. What's more important is what's on your plate consistently rather than being perfect each meal.

To better understand the BPM, let's break down each of the components.

PROTEIN

Protein is discussed a lot after weight-loss surgery, and for good reason. Protein consists of amino acids, which are the building blocks for your entire body. We tend to think of protein as a component of muscle, but protein is also part of your skin, hair, nails, hormones, soft tissue and enzymes. Without enough protein in your diet, you begin to lose muscle and hair and may develop a weakened immune system. Including protein on your plate is vital for your long-term health.

Here are some options that would count toward your protein in a meal:

Animal Sources

- Beef
- Cheese
- Chicken
- Fish
- Lamb
- Pork
- Shellfish
- Turkey

Plant Sources

- Beans
- Edamame
- Seitan
- Tempeh
- Tofu

If you're including 3 to 4 ounces (85 to 113 g) of a protein source at each meal, you'll be more likely to meet your daily protein goals.

NON-STARCHY VEGETABLES

Despite protein being the largest portion of your meal, non-starchy vegetables are important too. Non-starchy vegetables do not contain a significant amount of carbohydrates, and they provide fiber and crucial vitamins and minerals for your body. They also add flavor and can help you feel more satisfied with your meal. It's important to find vegetables that you enjoy after surgery.

Experiment with different ones and try various cooking methods such as roasting, steaming, grilling or adding to soups to decide how you like them best. Don't be surprised if your taste buds change—many people do report taste changes after bariatric surgery. Preparing vegetables in a variety of ways will increase your chances of enjoying them.

Here are some examples of non-starchy vegetables to include on your plate:

- Artichokes
- Beets
- Bell peppers
- Broccoli
- Brussels sprouts
- Carrots
- Cauliflower
- Celery
- Collard greens
- Cucumbers
- Lettuce
- Spinach
- Swiss chard
- Tomatoes
- Zucchini

It's typically suggested that non-starchy vegetables account for 30 percent of your meal. This equates to about 2 to 3 ounces (57 to 85 g) per meal.

CARBOHYDRATES

Many people believe that after weight-loss surgery, they're not allowed to include carbohydrates in their diet. This simply is not true. While the goal immediately after surgery is to meet protein needs, once protein needs are comfortably met, carbohydrates can be reintroduced into the diet.

Instead of eliminating carbohydrates, the goal is to choose high-quality carbohydrates rather than more processed carbohydrates like white bread or sweets. A high-quality carbohydrate will typically include fiber in it and be a whole food. If following the BPM, carbohydrates can easily be included in your diet.

Here are some examples of high-quality carbohydrates:

- Fruit (i.e., berries, watermelon, bananas, oranges, apples)
- Starchy vegetables (i.e., sweet potatoes, corn, legumes, winter squash)
- Whole grains (i.e., brown rice, quinoa, whole wheat)

Including a balanced approach to eating after bariatric surgery will help maximize your nutrition without feeling deprived.

Carbohydrate foods are about 20 percent of your meal, which equates to about 1 to 2 ounces (28 to 57 g) per meal.

meal prep containers

"What type of meal prep containers should I get?"

This is one of the top questions I receive. So, let's talk about it.

Purchasing cute containers is one of the fun parts of meal prepping. But with so many options out there, how do you know which ones to buy?

My best advice is to keep it simple.

Here are my biggest tips . . .

- Use 1 to 2 cups (240 to 480 ml) containers. Yes, they may be a bit large at first but your portions will expand with time, plus it will prevent food from spilling out if you're eating from the container.
- Use glass containers when you want to reheat your food in the microwave or oven. These are also great for freezing.
- Use Mason jars for salads or for pureed foods.
- Bento boxes are excellent (and fun!) for cold served foods like fruit and deli meats. My favorite brand is LunchBot.
- Use meal prep containers with leak-proof lids to prevent spills. These are also great for freezing. My favorite brands are Snapware and LocknLock.

tips for success

Aside from general nutrition guidance, there are also other ways to set yourself up for success after weight-loss surgery. Here are some of the top tips that I give my clients:

Eat Protein First

Meeting your daily protein goal is important for your long-term health. Improve your chances of meeting your protein goals by eating your protein first. This way if you become full, you've already eaten protein in your meal. It is not necessary to finish everything on your plate.

Eat Slowly

Eating slower will help your body recognize when you are satisfied. Aim for 20 to 30 minutes per meal. This may also prevent discomfort after eating.

Eat Small Bites

In addition to eating slowly, it's also important to take small bites and chew thoroughly. This will help you regulate when you know you're becoming satisfied so you don't become overly full.

Reach Your Water Goals

Drinking adequate amounts of water will improve your metabolism, prevent dehydration, flush out waste and improve your skin. Always carry a water bottle with you and set a timer to remember to drink water if you find it helpful. Most surgery centers recommend at least 64 ounces (1.9 L) of water daily.

Move Your Body

If cleared by your doctor, begin including an exercise regimen in your routine. This will help improve your metabolism and preserve your muscle mass as you lose weight. It will also help cultivate your mental health, which is a crucial component of your long-term success.

Take Your Vitamins

Continue your multivitamin regimen and any other supplements recommended by your surgery team. Your portion sizes are very small after surgery and your body will not absorb nutrients the way it used to. Taking your vitamins daily is vital to your long-term health.

Don't Drink with Your Meals

It's common practice after weight-loss surgery not to drink liquids with your meals. Drinking liquids with your meals may push the food through your stomach faster and may cause you to become hungrier sooner. Drinking liquid with your meals may cause heartburn. The general guideline is not to drink anything within 30 minutes of your meals.

bariatric meal plans

In the following pages, you will find bariatric meal plans, complete with grocery lists and suggested meal prep schedules. If you're new to meal prepping, it may be helpful to choose two to three meals a week to start with. As your skills build, your confidence will increase and you'll likely be able to prepare more meals in a single session. Each person has their own meal prepping style, and it's important you find yours. You may prefer to meal prep two meals a week, or you may prefer to prepare seven. You could also choose to only meal prep the vegetables and sauces, and that is fine too. It's all about finding what works for you.

week 1: pureed diet

As your new stomach heals, your doctor will slowly advance your diet to different textures to make sure you are tolerating food. First, you are typically on a liquid diet, then puree, then soft moist foods and lastly regular meals. Each doctor has their own protocol so it's important to follow your doctor's guidelines.

Once your doctor advances your diet to the pureed stage, you'll likely be eager to start eating real food. While you may be excited to introduce new foods into your regimen, you may also be apprehensive about a pureed texture. This is completely normal!

The pureed recipes in this cookbook are full of flavor and designed to help nourish your body while it heals. They consist mostly of protein, since protein is so vital for your recovery. One of the biggest challenges during this stage is tolerance. To help improve tolerance, make sure your meals are moist and eat very slowly.

And if you are still struggling with this phase, keep in mind it won't last forever. This phase will soon be a distant memory.

LENGTH OF THE PUREED DIET

Every surgery center has different guidelines. Generally, this stage can last anywhere from 1 week to 1 month after surgery. Please follow the specific guidelines from your surgery center.

PORTION SIZES

Many people are alarmed when they find that they can only eat one small bite during their first meal after surgery. This is completely normal. Within a week you will likely reach up to 1 to 2 tablespoons at a time. Then as the swelling goes down in your new pouch, you will be closer to ¼ cup around 1 month after surgery.

Please remember these are just basic guidelines and not goals. It is more important to listen to your body. If you are feeling any pressure or pain, this is a signal to stop. Everyone advances differently, and that's okay. Please contact your bariatric surgery center if you are concerned with your progress.

PUREED DIET MENU

This week's meal prep can all be done on your meal prep day or days, except for the Vanilla Chunky Monkey Protein Drink (page 47). I suggest making that fresh since it will taste better and can quickly be prepared.

I included the classic Single-Serving Ricotta Bake (page 118) meal in this week's menu but with my own twist. Each individual portion is stored in Mason jars and reheated in the microwave when you are ready to eat. It's so good, and I can't wait for you to try it.

My goal with this week's meal prep was to create meals that could easily be frozen if you are unable to eat it all. All the entrée meals can be frozen into ice cube trays or silicone ice molds to save for another time. If the entrée is too dry when you reheat it, add broth to make it moister.

week 1

Breakfast #1: Comforting Bone Broth (page 48)
Breakfast #2: Vanilla Chunky Monkey Protein Drink (page 47)
Entrée #1: Single-Serving Ricotta Bake (page 118)
Entrée #2: High-Protein Carrot Ginger Soup (page 122)
Entrée #3: Chicken Carrot Pea Mash (page 73)
Entrée #4: Black Bean Dip (page 125)
Snack #1: Watermelon Mint Popsicles (page 142)

Suggested Schedule

	Monday	Tuesday	Wednesday	Thursday	Friday	Saturday	Sunday
Breakfast	Comforting Bone Broth (page 48)	Vanilla Chunky Monkey Protein Drink (page 47)	Comforting Bone Broth (page 48)	Vanilla Chunky Monkey Protein Drink (page 47)	Comforting Bone Broth (page 48)	Vanilla Chunky Monkey Protein Drink (page 47)	Comforting Bone Broth (page 48)
Lunch	Single-Serving Ricotta Bake (page 118)	Black Bean Dip (page 125)	Single-Serving Ricotta Bake (page 118)	Chicken Carrot Pea Mash (page 73)	Chicken Carrot Pea Mash (page 73)	Chicken Carrot Pea Mash (page 73)	Chicken Carrot Pea Mash (page 73)
Snack	Watermelon Mint Popsicles (page 142)	Watermelon Mint Popsicles (page 142)	Watermelon Mint Popsicles (page 142)	Watermelon Mint Popsicles (page 142)	Watermelon Mint Popsicles (page 142)	Watermelon Mint Popsicles (page 142)	Watermelon Mint Popsicles (page 142)
Dinner	Black Bean Dip (page 125)	Single-Serving Ricotta Bake (page 118)	Black Bean Dip (page 125)	Single-Serving Ricotta Bake (page 118)	High-Protein Carrot Ginger Soup (page 122)	High-Protein Carrot Ginger Soup (page 122)	High-Protein Carrot Ginger Soup (page 122)

Shopping List

PRODUCE

- ☐ 6 mint sprigs (3 g)
- ☐ 1 tbsp (1 g) ginger
- ☐ 1 lime
- ☐ 1 cup (140 g) watermelon
- ☐ ½ onion (80 g)
- ☐ 8 oz (226 g) baby carrots

DAIRY/MEAT

- ☐ ½ cup (120 ml) low-fat Greek yogurt
- ☐ 3 cups (720 ml) unsweetened vanilla almond milk
- ☐ 1 cup (246 g) part-skim ricotta cheese
- ☐ 1 egg
- ☐ ¼ cup (25 g) Parmesan cheese
- ☐ 1 whole rotisserie chicken

PANTRY

- ☐ 2¼ cups (540 ml) chicken broth
- ☐ 1 (15-oz [425-g]) can black beans
- ☐ ½ cup (120 ml) sugar-free marinara sauce, smooth
- ☐ 2 tbsp (30 ml) apple cider vinegar
- ☐ ¼ cup + 2 tbsp (48 g) peanut butter powder
- ☐ 2 scoops (62 g) unflavored protein powder
- ☐ 3 scoops (93 g) vanilla protein powder

FROZEN

- ☐ ½ cup (65 g) peas and carrots

STAPLES

- ☐ Vanilla extract
- ☐ Extra virgin olive oil
- ☐ Dried parsley
- ☐ Italian seasoning
- ☐ Cumin
- ☐ Chili powder
- ☐ Salt
- ☐ Black pepper
- ☐ Bay leaves
- ☐ Cinnamon (optional)
- ☐ Stevia liquid (optional)

MEAL PREP SCHEDULE

Meal Prep Day #1

Prepare the infused water for the Watermelon Mint Popsicles (page 142) to allow the flavors to develop while preparing the rest of the meal prep.

Remove the chicken meat from the rotisserie chicken and set it aside to make this week's meal prep. If you have extra, you can freeze it in an airtight container until you're ready to use it or for up to 1 month. Use the bones of the chicken to prepare the Comforting Bone Broth (page 48).

Prepare the High-Protein Carrot Ginger Soup (page 122) and freeze it in ice cube trays for later in the week.

Prepare the Chicken Carrot Pea Mash (page 73) and freeze it in ice cube trays for later in the week.

Prepare the Single-Serving Ricotta Bake (page 118).

Prepare the Black Bean Dip (page 125).

Prepare the Watermelon Mint Popsicles (page 142).

The Vanilla Chunky Monkey Protein Drink (page 47) will be prepared fresh.

week 2: soft food diet

You made it to the soft food diet stage! Chances are you're eager to start eating food with texture, but you want to eat the right foods to optimize your weight loss and prevent complications such as nausea. This week's meal prep was designed with you in mind.

LENGTH OF THE SOFT FOOD DIET

Each surgery center provides different guidance on how long to follow the soft food diet. It's important to follow yours. It's usually around 2 to 4 weeks.

PORTION SIZES

The swelling in your stomach has gone down by the time you reach this stage, so you can likely tolerate more food. Portions at this time are generally around ¼ to ½ cup (60 to 120 ml) portions. Each person is different, and it's important to do what is best for you and within your doctor's guidelines.

SOFT FOOD DIET MENU

This week's menu plan has more soup-like recipes to help improve your tolerance since they are moist. The entrées can also be frozen if you are unable to eat all the quantities the recipe provides. Each person is a little different, so it's important to listen to what your body needs.

All the meals can be prepped ahead of time—however, I suggest preparing the Quick Indian Lentil Soup (page 121) fresh and then eating the leftovers throughout the week. This will lessen your workload on your meal prep day since it's so easy to prepare.

My favorite meal this week is the Egg Drop Soup (page 126). It has a savory flavor and tastes like it is from a restaurant. You may also enjoy the Easy Parmesan Crisps (page 141). They are super easy to prepare, and you can add toppings to them once your diet progresses.

week 2

Breakfast #1: Peachy Cottage Cheese (page 51)

Breakfast #2: Mini Muffin Ham Frittatas (page 52)

Entrée #1: Egg Drop Soup (page 126)

Entrée #2: Tuscan Chicken & White Bean Soup (page 74)

Entrée #3: Quick Indian Lentil Soup (page 121)

Entrée #4: Simple Chicken Salad (page 77)

Snack #1: Easy Parmesan Crisps (page 141)

Suggested Schedule

	Monday	Tuesday	Wednesday	Thursday	Friday	Saturday	Sunday
Breakfast	Peachy Cottage Cheese (page 51)	Peachy Cottage Cheese (page 51)	Peachy Cottage Cheese (page 51)	Mini Muffin Ham Frittatas (page 52)	Mini Muffin Ham Frittatas (page 52)	Mini Muffin Ham Frittatas (page 52)	Peachy Cottage Cheese (page 51)
Lunch	Egg Drop Soup (page 126)	Egg Drop Soup (page 126)	Egg Drop Soup (page 126)	Egg Drop Soup (page 126)	Simple Chicken Salad (page 77)	Simple Chicken Salad (page 77)	Simple Chicken Salad (page 77)
Snack	Easy Parmesan Crisps (page 141)	Easy Parmesan Crisps (page 141)	Easy Parmesan Crisps (page 141)	Easy Parmesan Crisps (page 141)	Easy Parmesan Crisps (page 141)	Easy Parmesan Crisps (page 141)	Easy Parmesan Crisps (page 141)
Dinner	Tuscan Chicken & White Bean Soup (page 74)	Quick Indian Lentil Soup (page 121)	Tuscan Chicken & White Bean Soup (page 74)	Quick Indian Lentil Soup (page 121)	Tuscan Chicken & White Bean Soup (page 74)	Quick Indian Lentil Soup (page 121)	Quick Indian Lentil Soup (page 121)

Shopping List

PRODUCE

- [ ] 1 carrot (60 g)
- [ ] 1 zucchini (200 g)
- [ ] 1 celery rib (50 g)
- [ ] 1 cup (30 g) spinach
- [ ] 1 onion (250 g)

DAIRY/MEAT

- [ ] 12 eggs
- [ ] 1 cup (240 ml) low-fat cottage cheese
- [ ] ¼ cup (60 ml) low-fat milk
- [ ] 3 oz (85 g) Parmesan cheese
- [ ] 2 oz (57 g) ham
- [ ] 8 oz (226 g) rotisserie chicken meat

FROZEN

- [ ] 1 cup (135 g) peas and carrots

PANTRY

- [ ] 4 oz (113 g) canned fire-roasted green peppers
- [ ] 9½ cups (2.2 L) chicken broth
- [ ] 1 (14-oz [397-g]) can cannellini beans
- [ ] 2 (15-oz [425-g]) cans lentils
- [ ] 1 (12-oz [340-g]) can chicken
- [ ] ½ cup (124 g) canned peaches
- [ ] 3 tbsp (45 ml) reduced-fat mayonnaise

STAPLES

- [ ] Salt
- [ ] Black pepper
- [ ] Ground ginger
- [ ] Garlic powder
- [ ] Onion powder
- [ ] Toasted sesame oil
- [ ] Dried thyme
- [ ] Dried rosemary
- [ ] White wine vinegar
- [ ] Extra virgin olive oil
- [ ] Indian curry powder
- [ ] Celery seed
- [ ] Reduced-sodium soy sauce
- [ ] Cinnamon

MEAL PREP SCHEDULE

Meal Prep Day #1

Prepare the Tuscan Chicken & White Bean Soup (page 74).

Prepare the Mini Muffin Ham Frittatas (page 52).

Prepare the Egg Drop Soup (page 126).

Prepare the Easy Parmesan Crisps (page 141).

Prepare the Peachy Cottage Cheese (page 51).

Meal Prep Day #2

Prepare the Simple Chicken Salad (page 77).

The Quick Indian Lentil Soup (page 121) may be prepared fresh.

week 3: regular diet

Hooray!

You've now entered the regular diet stage. Chances are you probably have mixed emotions. You want to include more variety in your diet, but you don't want to include foods that may inhibit your progress.

It can feel intimidating when your doctor says, "Okay, all foods are now allowed." This is why I wrote this cookbook—to provide you with a general idea of what a healthy diet can look like after weight-loss surgery. You can incorporate a variety of foods, and correct portions will help you reach your health goals.

REGULAR DIET MENU

As you begin eating a regular diet, it's important to remember that each person is different, and your portion sizes may not be very large yet, despite entering the regular stage. Adapt the recipes to fit your personal needs. This week's menu has more of a Mediterranean theme and includes fresh fish, chickpeas and tomatoes.

All the meals may be prepared ahead of time, but it's okay if you do not prepare them all on the same day. In fact, you may enjoy some of the food more freshly prepared, such as the Chorizo Egg Scramble (page 44), Grilled Pork Tenderloin with Balsamic Apple Topping (page 94) and Sheet Pan Pesto Trout with Roasted Tomatoes (page 106). You also will not have to spend all day in the kitchen if you break it up. I typically suggest two meal prep days per week. One on Sunday that preps for Monday through Wednesday and another on Wednesday that preps for Thursday through Sunday.

My favorite recipes this week include the Grilled Pork Tenderloin with Balsamic Apple Topping (page 94) and the Frozen Mini Chocolate Peanut Butter Cups (page 146). I also love the Falafel Lettuce Wraps (page 129)—you can even make extra this week and freeze them for another time. They are so good!

You can also use the Red Pepper Hummus (page 134) in the Falafel Lettuce Wraps (page 129) recipe.

week 3

Breakfast #1: Apple Pie Parfait (page 55)

Breakfast #2: Chorizo Egg Scramble (page 44)

Entrée #1: Chicken Walnut Mason Jar Salad (page 78)

Entrée #2: Falafel Lettuce Wraps with Hummus (page 129)

Entrée #3: Grilled Pork Tenderloin with Balsamic Apple Topping (page 94)

Entrée #4: Sheet Pan Pesto Trout with Roasted Tomatoes (page 106)

Snack #1: Blueberry Coconut Trail Mix (page 145)

Snack #2: Red Pepper Hummus with Baby Carrots (page 134)

Snack #3: Frozen Mini Chocolate Peanut Butter Cups (page 146)

Suggested Schedule

	Monday	Tuesday	Wednesday	Thursday	Friday	Saturday	Sunday
Breakfast	Apple Pie Parfait (page 55)	Apple Pie Parfait (page 55)	Chorizo Egg Scramble (page 44)	Chorizo Egg Scramble (page 44)	Chorizo Egg Scramble (page 44)	Apple Pie Parfait (page 55)	Apple Pie Parfait (page 55)
Lunch	Chicken Walnut Mason Jar Salad (page 78)	Chicken Walnut Mason Jar Salad (page 78)	Chicken Walnut Mason Jar Salad (page 78)	Chicken Walnut Mason Jar Salad (page 78)	Falafel Lettuce Wraps with Hummus (page 129)	Falafel Lettuce Wraps with Hummus (page 129)	Falafel Lettuce Wraps with Hummus (page 129)
Snack	Blueberry Coconut Trail Mix (page 145)	Blueberry Coconut Trail Mix (page 145)	Blueberry Coconut Trail Mix (page 145)	Blueberry Coconut Trail Mix (page 145)	Red Pepper Hummus with Baby Carrots (page 134)	Red Pepper Hummus with Baby Carrots (page 134)	Frozen Mini Chocolate Peanut Butter Cups (page 146)
Dinner	Sheet Pan Pesto Trout with Roasted Tomatoes (page 106)	Sheet Pan Pesto Trout with Roasted Tomatoes (page 106)	Sheet Pan Pesto Trout with Roasted Tomatoes (page 106)	Falafel Lettuce Wraps with Hummus (page 129)	Grilled Pork Tenderloin with Balsamic Apple Topping (page 94)	Grilled Pork Tenderloin with Balsamic Apple Topping (page 94)	Grilled Pork Tenderloin with Balsamic Apple Topping (page 94)

Shopping List

PRODUCE

- [ ] 4 apples (720 g)
- [ ] 2 cups (296 g) blueberries
- [ ] 1 cup (150 g) red grapes
- [ ] 1 onion (250 g)
- [ ] 1 red onion (250 g)
- [ ] 6 cloves garlic
- [ ] 2¼ cups (340 g) grape tomatoes
- [ ] 1 celery rib (50 g)
- [ ] 1½ cups (165 g) baby carrots
- [ ] 1 head lettuce (300 g)
- [ ] ½ cup (30 g) parsley
- [ ] 1 bunch cilantro

DAIRY/MEAT/REFRIGERATED

- [ ] 4 eggs
- [ ] ½ cup (120 ml) hummus
- [ ] 2 cups (480 ml) plain low-fat Greek yogurt
- [ ] 1 chorizo chicken sausage (85 g)
- [ ] 12 oz (340 g) rotisserie chicken meat
- [ ] 1 lb (454 g) pork tenderloin
- [ ] 1 lb (454 g) skin-on trout

PANTRY

- [ ] ¼ cup (28 g) pecans
- [ ] ¼ cup (14 g) walnuts
- [ ] ¾ cup (109 g) raw cashews
- [ ] 2 (15-oz [425-g]) cans chickpeas
- [ ] 1 cup (260 g) roasted red bell peppers
- [ ] ½ cup (113 g) pesto
- [ ] ½ cup (85 g) quinoa
- [ ] ½ cup (47 g) unsweetened shredded coconut
- [ ] 8 oz (226 g) sugar-free chocolate chips
- [ ] ¼ cup (32 g) peanut butter powder

STAPLES

- [ ] Balsamic vinegar
- [ ] Extra virgin olive oil
- [ ] Dijon mustard
- [ ] Honey
- [ ] Apple spice
- [ ] Cumin
- [ ] Cardamom
- [ ] Salt
- [ ] Black pepper
- [ ] Italian seasoning

MEAL PREP SCHEDULE

Meal Prep Day #1

Prep the Falafel Lettuce Wraps (page 129). You can either choose to prepare the entire dish or just the falafels. Once you prepare the falafels, keep them in an airtight container separate from the lettuce for up to 4 days. Then when you're ready to eat, place the falafels in the lettuce wrap and top with hummus.

Prep the Chorizo Egg Scramble (page 44). You can either choose to prepare the entire dish or pre-cut the ingredients. To pre-cut the ingredients, chop ¼ cup (50 g) onion, slice ¼ cup (40 g) grape tomatoes in half and slice 1 chorizo chicken sausage. Store them separately in airtight containers until ready to use.

Prepare the Chicken Walnut Mason Jar Salad (page 78).

Prepare the Sheet Pan Pesto Trout with Roasted Tomatoes (page 106).

Prepare one batch of the Apple Pie Parfait (page 55).

(continued)

Prepare the Blueberry Coconut Trail Mix (page 145).

Prepare the Red Pepper Hummus with Baby Carrots (page 134).

Meal Prep Day #2

Prepare the Grilled Pork Tenderloin with Apple Balsamic Topping (page 94).

Prepare the Frozen Chocolate Peanut Butter Cups (page 146). If you don't eat all of the peanut butter cups this week, then you can store them in the freezer for up to 1 month.

Prepare a second batch of the Apple Pie Parfait (page 55).

week 4: regular diet

REGULAR DIET MENU

This week I'm delivering some delicious options to you. This week's menu includes Mexican-inspired meals, like the Chicken Fajita Bowl (page 82) and the Taco-Stuffed Zucchini Boats (page 81).

All of these are easy to prepare, and you will want to make them again and again. I am introducing chia seeds this week, which you can incorporate into your diet for healthy bowel regularity.

All the meals can easily be prepped ahead of time, but the Zucchini Pizza Bites (page 137) taste so good fresh.

week 4

Breakfast #1: High-Protein Oatmeal Pancakes (page 56)
Breakfast #2: Ham & Egg Cups (page 59)
Entrée #1: Mini Meatloaf with Broccoli (page 97)
Entrée #2: Taco-Stuffed Zucchini Boats (page 81)
Entrée #3: Chicken Fajita Bowl (page 82)
Entrée #4: Mason Jar Cobb Salad (page 85)
Snack #1: Zucchini Pizza Bites (page 137)
Snack #2: Raspberry Dark Chocolate Chia Seed Pudding (page 149)
Snack #3: Lime Chia Seed Pudding (page 150)

Suggested Schedule

	Monday	Tuesday	Wednesday	Thursday	Friday	Saturday	Sunday
Breakfast	High-Protein Oatmeal Pancakes (page 56)	High-Protein Oatmeal Pancakes (page 56)	High-Protein Oatmeal Pancakes (page 56)	High-Protein Oatmeal Pancakes (page 56)	Ham & Egg Cups (page 59)	Ham & Egg Cups (page 59)	Ham & Egg Cups (page 59)
Lunch	Chicken Fajita Bowl (page 82)	Chicken Fajita Bowl (page 82)	Chicken Fajita Bowl (page 82)	Chicken Fajita Bowl (page 82)	Mason Jar Cobb Salad (page 85)	Mason Jar Cobb Salad (page 85)	Mason Jar Cobb Salad (page 85)
Snack	Zucchini Pizza Bites (page 137)	Zucchini Pizza Bites (page 137)	Zucchini Pizza Bites (page 137)	Lime Chia Seed Pudding (page 150)	Lime Chia Seed Pudding (page 150)	Raspberry Dark Chocolate Chia Seed Pudding (page 149)	Raspberry Dark Chocolate Chia Seed Pudding (page 149)
Dinner	Mini Meatloaf with Broccoli (page 97)	Mini Meatloaf with Broccoli (page 97)	Mini Meatloaf with Broccoli (page 97)	Mini Meatloaf with Broccoli (page 97)	Taco-Stuffed Zucchini Boats (page 81)	Taco-Stuffed Zucchini Boats (page 81)	Taco-Stuffed Zucchini Boats (page 81)

Shopping List

PRODUCE

- [ ] 1 banana (130 g)
- [ ] ½ cup (83 g) strawberries
- [ ] 3 mandarins (275 g)
- [ ] ½ cup (62 g) raspberries
- [ ] 2 limes
- [ ] 2 onions (500 g)
- [ ] 1 red bell pepper (150 g)
- [ ] ½ cucumber (100 g)
- [ ] 1 plum tomato (60 g)
- [ ] 1½ cups (140 g) broccoli
- [ ] 3 medium zucchinis (600 g)
- [ ] 1½ cups (55 g) chopped lettuce
- [ ] 1 bunch cilantro

DAIRY/MEAT/REFRIGERATED

- [ ] 1¼ cups (600 ml) low-fat milk
- [ ] ½ cup (120 ml) almond milk
- [ ] ½ cup (120 ml) plain low-fat Greek yogurt
- [ ] 10 eggs
- [ ] ⅔ cup (75 g) cheddar cheese
- [ ] ¼ cup (34 g) bleu cheese
- [ ] ½ cup (50 g) mozzarella
- [ ] 8 oz (226 g) rotisserie chicken meat
- [ ] 1 lb (454 g) chicken breasts
- [ ] 1 lb (454 g) lean ground turkey
- [ ] 1½ lb (680 g) lean ground beef
- [ ] 9 slices (150 g) Canadian bacon

PANTRY

- [ ] 1⅓ cups (110 g) rolled oats
- [ ] ⅓ cup (35 g) breadcrumbs
- [ ] ¼ cup (60 ml) ketchup
- [ ] 2 tbsp (32 g) tomato paste
- [ ] 1 (15-oz [425-g]) can black beans
- [ ] ½ cup (120 ml) sugar-free marinara sauce
- [ ] 6 tbsp (60 g) chia seeds
- [ ] 3 tbsp (20 g) cocoa powder
- [ ] 1 tbsp (16 g) almond butter
- [ ] 1 tbsp (15 ml) sugar-free maple syrup
- [ ] ½ scoop (15 g) vanilla protein powder
- [ ] 2 tbsp (16 g) peanut butter powder

STAPLES

- [ ] Vanilla extract
- [ ] Cinnamon
- [ ] Celery seed
- [ ] Onion powder
- [ ] Salt
- [ ] Black pepper
- [ ] Parsley flakes
- [ ] Chili powder
- [ ] Cumin
- [ ] Garlic powder
- [ ] Oregano
- [ ] Italian seasoning
- [ ] Extra virgin olive oil
- [ ] White wine vinegar
- [ ] Dijon mustard

Meal Prep Day #1

Prepare the hard-boiled eggs. Boil water in a saucepan over medium heat and gently add 2 eggs. Boil for 10 minutes. Remove the eggs from the hot water and store them in the refrigerator for later in the week to use in the Mason Jar Cobb Salad (page 85).

Prepare the Mini Meatloaf with Broccoli (page 97). You can prepare the entire meal or just prep the meatloaves.

Prepare the Chicken Fajita Bowl (page 82).

Prepare the High-Protein Oatmeal Pancakes (page 56). You can prepare the entire meal or just prep the batter and store it in the refrigerator for up to 4 days and then prepare the pancakes fresh.

Slice up the zucchini for the Zucchini Pizza Bites (page 137) and store the slices in an airtight container for up to 4 days, until you're ready to prepare the entire snack.

Prepare the Raspberry Dark Chocolate Chia Seed Pudding (page 149).

Meal Prep Day #2

Prepare the Taco-Stuffed Zucchini Boats (page 81). You can prepare the entire meal or just prepare the meat mixture and the zucchini boats.

Prepare the Ham & Egg Cups (page 59).

Prepare the Mason Jar Cobb Salad (page 85).

Prepare the Lime Chia Seed Pudding (page 150).

week 5: regular diet

REGULAR DIET MENU

In this week's menu, I am introducing you to Single-Serving Chicken Pot Pies (page 86). I love this idea because these small, individual servings will help keep your portion sizes within the proper guidelines. You can use this recipe as a jumping-off point for other recipe ideas that involve using a wonton wrapper.

I also introduce a shrimp dish. I love including shrimp in my meal prep because they are quick to prepare and a good protein source.

week 5

Breakfast #1: Strawberry Cheesecake Overnight Oats (page 43)

Breakfast #2: Breakfast Salad (page 60)

Entrée #1: Blackened Salmon with Mango Salsa & Roasted Cauliflower (page 109)

Entrée #2: Single-Serving Chicken Pot Pies (page 86)

Entrée #3: Enchilada-Stuffed Bell Peppers (page 70)

Entrée #4: Tropical Shrimp Ceviche (page 110)

Snack #1: Caprese Salad (page 153)

Snack #2: Carrot Spice Mini Muffins (page 154)

Snack #3: Sweet Balsamic Strawberries & Mint (page 157)

Suggested Schedule

	Monday	Tuesday	Wednesday	Thursday	Friday	Saturday	Sunday
Breakfast	Strawberry Cheesecake Overnight Oats (page 43)	Strawberry Cheesecake Overnight Oats (page 43)	Breakfast Salad (page 60)	Breakfast Salad (page 60)	Breakfast Salad (page 60)	Strawberry Cheesecake Overnight Oats (page 43)	Strawberry Cheesecake Overnight Oats (page 43)
Lunch	Single-Serving Chicken Pot Pies (page 86)	Single-Serving Chicken Pot Pies (page 86)	Single-Serving Chicken Pot Pies (page 86)	Single-Serving Chicken Pot Pies (page 86)	Tropical Shrimp Ceviche (page 110)	Tropical Shrimp Ceviche (page 110)	Tropical Shrimp Ceviche (page 110)
Snack	Sweet Balsamic Strawberries & Mint (page 157)	Sweet Balsamic Strawberries & Mint (page 157)	Sweet Balsamic Strawberries & Mint (page 157)	Caprese Salad (page 153)	Caprese Salad (page 153)	Caprese Salad (page 153)	Carrot Spice Mini Muffins (page 154)
Dinner	Blackened Salmon with Mango Salsa & Roasted Cauliflower (page 109)	Blackened Salmon with Mango Salsa & Roasted Cauliflower (page 109)	Blackened Salmon with Mango Salsa & Roasted Cauliflower (page 109)	Enchilada-Stuffed Bell Peppers (page 70)	Enchilada-Stuffed Bell Peppers (page 70)	Enchilada-Stuffed Bell Peppers (page 70)	Enchilada-Stuffed Bell Peppers (page 70)

Shopping List

PRODUCE

- [ ] 1½ cups (315 g) strawberries
- [ ] 2 mangoes (300 g)
- [ ] 1 banana (130 g)
- [ ] 3 limes
- [ ] 3 lemons
- [ ] 2 onions (500 g)
- [ ] 2 red onions (500 g)
- [ ] 1 Roma tomato (60 g)
- [ ] 3 cups (500 g) cherry tomatoes
- [ ] 2 green bell peppers (300 g)
- [ ] 2 avocados (300 g)
- [ ] 1½ cups (150 g) cauliflower
- [ ] 2 carrots (100 g)
- [ ] 6 basil leaves (6 g)
- [ ] 1 tbsp (1 g) mint
- [ ] 2 bunches cilantro

DAIRY/MEAT/FISH/REFRIGERATED

- [ ] ¼ cup (57 g) butter
- [ ] 1¼ cups (360 ml) low-fat milk
- [ ] ¾ cup (180 ml) plain low-fat Greek yogurt
- [ ] ¼ cup (28 g) cheddar cheese
- [ ] 8 oz (226 g) mozzarella balls
- [ ] 1 cup (246 g) part-skim ricotta cheese
- [ ] 7 eggs
- [ ] 8 oz (226 g) rotisserie chicken meat, shredded
- [ ] 4 cooked chicken sausage breakfast links (90 g)
- [ ] 1 lb (454 g) lean ground turkey
- [ ] 12 oz (340 g) salmon, skin removed
- [ ] 12 oz (340 g) cooked shrimp
- [ ] 12 wonton wrappers

FROZEN

- [ ] 1 cup (135 g) peas and carrots

PANTRY

- [ ] 1 cup (40 g) rolled oats
- [ ] ¼ cup (30 g) flour
- [ ] 1 cup (95 g) almond flour
- [ ] ¼ cup (32 g) coconut flour
- [ ] 1 tsp baking soda
- [ ] 1 tbsp (10 g) chia seeds
- [ ] 2 tbsp (30 ml) maple syrup
- [ ] 1 cup (240 ml) chicken broth
- [ ] 2 cups (480 ml) enchilada sauce

STAPLES

- [ ] Paprika
- [ ] Onion powder
- [ ] Garlic powder
- [ ] Dried oregano
- [ ] Salt
- [ ] Black pepper
- [ ] Cinnamon
- [ ] Extra virgin olive oil
- [ ] Balsamic vinegar

MEAL PREP SCHEDULE

Meal Prep Day #1

Prepare one batch of the Strawberry Cheesecake Overnight Oats (page 43) and store them in the refrigerator for up to 3 days.

Prepare the Blackened Salmon with Mango Salsa & Roasted Cauliflower (page 109). Prepare the entire meal or cut up 1½ cups (150 g) cauliflower florets and prep the mango salsa. Store them separately in airtight containers until you're ready to prepare the entire meal.

Prepare the Single-Serving Chicken Pot Pies (page 86).

(continued)

Prepare the Sweet Balsamic Strawberries & Mint (page 157) and store them in the refrigerator for up to 3 days.

Prepare the Carrot Spice Mini Muffins (page 154) and store them in an airtight container in the freezer until you're ready to eat them. They will keep frozen for up to 1 month.

Meal Prep Day #2

Prepare the Breakfast Salad (page 60) and store it in the refrigerator for up to 3 days.

Prepare the Tropical Shrimp Ceviche (page 110) and store it in the refrigerator for up to 3 days.

Prepare the Enchilada-Stuffed Bell Peppers (page 70). Prepare the entire meal or prep the meat mixture and cut the bell peppers in half and remove the seeds. Store them in separate containers until you're ready to prepare the entire meal.

Prepare the Caprese Salad (page 153) and store it in the refrigerator for up to 3 days.

Prepare a second batch of the Strawberry Cheesecake Overnight Oats (page 43) and store them in the refrigerator for up to 3 days.

week 6: regular diet

REGULAR DIET MENU

To make meal prep easier this week, the recipes included in this meal plan have an Italian theme. Marinara sauce, Italian seasoning and Parmesan cheese are used throughout the week in meals such as Zoodles & Meatballs (page 89) and Chicken Parmesan & Sautéed Zucchini (page 66).

If you enjoy crab cakes, you'll love the Salmon Cake Bento Box (page 113) this week. They are simple to prepare and are perfect for a grab-and-go meal. I also want to highlight the Apple & Peanut Butter Dip (page 162) snack. It's so good, and I am so excited to share it with you.

week 6

Breakfast #1: Pineapple Green Smoothie (page 40)

Breakfast #2: Savory Oats (page 63)

Entrée #1: Zoodles & Meatballs (page 89)

Entrée #2: Chicken Parmesan & Sautéed Zucchini (page 66)

Entrée #3: Lemon Herb Pork Chops & Roasted Brussels Sprouts (page 98)

Entrée #4: Salmon Cake Bento Box (page 113)

Snack #1: Parmesan-Roasted Edamame (page 158)

Snack #2: High-Protein Berry Popsicles (page 161)

Snack #3: Apple & Peanut Butter Dip (page 162)

Suggested Schedule

	Monday	Tuesday	Wednesday	Thursday	Friday	Saturday	Sunday
Breakfast	Savory Oats (page 63)	Savory Oats (page 63)	Savory Oats (page 63)	Pineapple Green Smoothie (page 40)	Pineapple Green Smoothie (page 40)	Pineapple Green Smoothie (page 40)	Pineapple Green Smoothie (page 40)
Lunch	Zoodles & Meatballs (page 89)	Zoodles & Meatballs (page 89)	Zoodles & Meatballs (page 89)	Zoodles & Meatballs (page 89)	Salmon Cake Bento Box (page 113)	Salmon Cake Bento Box (page 113)	Salmon Cake Bento Box (page 113)
Snack	Parmesan-Roasted Edamame (page 158)	Parmesan-Roasted Edamame (page 158)	Parmesan-Roasted Edamame (page 158)	Parmesan-Roasted Edamame (page 158)	Apple & Peanut Butter Dip (page 162)	Apple & Peanut Butter Dip (page 162)	High-Protein Berry Popsicles (page 161)
Dinner	Lemon Herb Pork Chops & Roasted Brussels Sprouts (page 98)	Lemon Herb Pork Chops & Roasted Brussels Sprouts (page 98)	Lemon Herb Pork Chops & Roasted Brussels Sprouts (page 98)	Lemon Herb Pork Chops & Roasted Brussels Sprouts (page 98)	Chicken Parmesan & Sautéed Zucchini (page 66)	Chicken Parmesan & Sautéed Zucchini (page 66)	Chicken Parmesan & Sautéed Zucchini (page 66)

Shopping List

PRODUCE

- [ ] 1 apple (180 g)
- [ ] 1 banana (130 g)
- [ ] 1 lemon
- [ ] 2 green onions (30 g)
- [ ] 4 zucchinis (800 g)
- [ ] 1½ cups (132 g) Brussels sprouts
- [ ] 1 green bell pepper (150 g)
- [ ] 1 medium cucumber (200 g)
- [ ] 2 cups (60 g) spinach

DAIRY/MEAT/FISH/REFRIGERATED

- [ ] 3 cups (720 ml) almond milk
- [ ] 1 cup (240 ml) + 1 tbsp (15 ml) low-fat Greek yogurt
- [ ] ⅔ cup (360 ml) low-fat vanilla Greek yogurt
- [ ] 6 eggs
- [ ] 1¼ cups (125 g) Parmesan cheese
- [ ] 2 oz (57 g) mozzarella
- [ ] 1 slice (11 g) turkey bacon
- [ ] 1 lb (454 g) chicken tenders
- [ ] 1 lb (454 g) thinly sliced pork chops

FROZEN

- [ ] 2 cups (280 g) pineapple
- [ ] 1 cup (150 g) berries
- [ ] 10 oz (283 g) shelled edamame
- [ ] 12 oz (340 g) cooked turkey meatballs

PANTRY

- [ ] ¾ cup (40 g) rolled oats
- [ ] 2 cups (110 g) whole wheat panko
- [ ] 1 tsp Old Bay Seasoning
- [ ] 5 scoops (60 g) vanilla protein powder
- [ ] ¼ cup (32 g) peanut butter powder
- [ ] ¼ cup (41 g) chia seeds
- [ ] 1 cup (240 ml) applesauce
- [ ] 2 (5-oz [142-g]) cans of salmon
- [ ] 2 (24-oz [680-g]) jars sugar-free marinara sauce

STAPLES

- [ ] Extra virgin olive oil
- [ ] Maple syrup
- [ ] Vanilla extract
- [ ] Salt
- [ ] Black pepper
- [ ] Cayenne pepper
- [ ] Oregano

MEAL PREP SCHEDULE

Meal Prep Day #1

Prepare the Savory Oats (page 63). Prepare the entire meal, or only the oatmeal, and cut up the green onions. Store them separately in airtight containers for up to 3 days.

Prepare the Zoodles & Meatballs (page 89). I suggest preparing the entire meal, since it will be used as lunch this week.

Prepare the Lemon Herb Pork Chops & Roasted Brussels Sprouts (page 98). Prepare the entire meal or only clean and cut the Brussels sprouts and store them in an airtight container until you're ready to prepare the entire meal.

Prepare the Parmesan-Roasted Edamame (page 158) and High-Protein Berry Popsicles (page 161).

Meal Prep Day #2

Prepare the Chicken Parmesan & Sautéed Zucchini (page 66). Prepare the entire meal or only clean and cut the zucchini and store it in an airtight container until you're ready to prepare the entire meal.

Prepare the Salmon Cake Bento Box (page 113) and Apple & Peanut Butter Dip (page 162).

Prepare the Pineapple Green Smoothie (page 40). Divide the dry ingredients into ziplock freezer bags and store them in the freezer until you are ready to add your liquid and drink fresh.

breakfast

You've likely heard that eating breakfast is important, but it's even more imperative to do so after weight-loss surgery. When you don't have breakfast, you're more likely to miss your daily protein goals. In the following pages, you will find lots of inspiration to start your day off with a high-protein breakfast.

Pineapple Green Smoothie

Once someone reaches the regular diet stage, generally they can begin to include fruit in their protein drinks for added fiber and nutrients. In this recipe, I used about ¾ cup (105 g) of pineapple and banana in each serving to add flavor without overloading your body with sugar. You can adjust to your needs. I also added spinach to this protein drink to give you an opportunity to get in more veggies.

Yield: 4 (16-oz [480-ml]) servings

Total Prep Time: 5 minutes

Suggested Stage: Regular

To Prep

2 cups (280 g) frozen pineapple

1 banana (130 g), sliced into fourths

2 cups (60 g) spinach

¼ cup (40 g) chia seeds

4 scoops (124 g) vanilla protein powder (I use Isopure)

To Serve

3 cups (720 ml) almond milk

In four ziplock freezer bags, evenly divide the pineapple, banana, spinach, chia seeds and protein powder. This works out to be about ½ cup (70 g) of pineapple, ¼ (30 g) of a banana, ½ cup (15 g) of spinach, 1 tablespoon (10 g) of chia seeds and 1 scoop (31 g) of vanilla protein powder in each bag. Freeze for up to 1 month, until ready to serve.

To make one serving: Place the contents of one bag in a blender and add ¾ cup (180 ml) of almond milk. Blend until smooth and enjoy!

Nutrition Per Serving

Calories: 249, Fat: 5.5 g, Carbohydrates: 23.5 g, Fiber: 5.7 g, Protein: 29 g

Strawberry Cheesecake Overnight Oats

Overnight oats are an easy meal prep breakfast to incorporate into your routine. Oatmeal is high in fiber but can lack protein after weight-loss surgery. To help boost the protein in this meal, I added Greek yogurt as a topping. These can be stored in Mason jars.

Makes: 2 servings

Total Prep Time: 5 minutes

Suggested Stage: Regular

½ cup (20 g) rolled oats

½ cup (120 ml) low-fat milk

¼ cup (42 g) sliced strawberries

¼ cup (60 ml) low-fat Greek yogurt

Add ¼ cup (10 g) of rolled oats and ¼ cup (60 ml) of milk to each Mason jar. Top each with 2 tablespoons (21 g) of sliced strawberries and 2 tablespoons (30 ml) of Greek yogurt. Store them in the refrigerator overnight or for up to 3 days.

Notes: *You can add peanut butter powder to increase the protein.*

If this portion size does not fill you up, then you can double the recipe to fit your needs.

Nutrition Per Serving
Calories: 129, Fat: 1.2 g, Carbohydrates: 19.2 g, Protein: 7.7 g

Chorizo Egg Scramble

Chorizo is a spicy Spanish pork sausage that makes a delicious breakfast meat. This dish uses a chicken sausage option instead to reduce unnecessary fat after surgery, but it still has loads of flavor. I suggest adding fresh fruit such as strawberries on the side.

Makes: 3 servings

Total Prep Time: 15 minutes

Suggested Stage: Regular

1 tsp olive oil

1 chorizo chicken/turkey sausage or chicken sausage of your choice (I use Aidells)

¼ cup (50 g) chopped onion

4 eggs

½ cup (130 g) roasted bell peppers

¼ cup (10 g) chopped cilantro

¼ cup (40 g) grape tomatoes, sliced in half

Heat the olive oil over medium heat in a medium skillet. While heating, slice the chorizo chicken sausage. Once the skillet is hot, add the onion and sauté it for 5 minutes.

Next, add the sliced sausage and cook for another 2 minutes. While cooking, whisk together the eggs.

Once the sausage is warmed through, add the eggs to the mixture. Cook until the eggs are cooked all the way through, 2 to 3 minutes. Then add the roasted bell peppers.

Remove the skillet from the heat. Divide the scramble into meal prep containers. Reheat it in the microwave in 30-second intervals. Add the cilantro and grape tomatoes right before serving.

Note: *Serve with fresh fruit or a corn tortilla on the side for a balanced meal.*

Nutrition Per Serving
Calories: 178, Fat: 11.7 g, Carbohydrates: 4.4 g, Fiber: 1.3 g, Protein: 13.6 g

Vanilla Chunky Monkey Protein Drink

Vanilla protein powder is a great base for homemade protein drinks or to boost the protein content in smoothies. In this recipe, I added peanut butter powder, but you could also add cocoa powder. I typically suggest using a protein powder that has more than 20 grams of protein per serving and less than 5 grams of carbohydrates. I used Isopure for this recipe. This protein drink tastes best when prepared right before drinking.

Makes: 1 serving

Total Prep Time: 5 minutes

Suggested Stages: Pureed, Soft, Regular

8 oz (240 ml) unsweetened vanilla almond milk

1 scoop (29 g) vanilla protein powder

2 tbsp (16 g) peanut butter powder

1 tsp cinnamon (optional)

Place all the ingredients into a blender and blend until smooth. Enjoy immediately.

Note: *The nutrition per serving was calculated using almond milk.*

Nutrition Per Serving
Calories: 209, Fat: 4.9 g, Carbohydrate: 6.5 g, Fiber: 3 g, Protein: 34.5 g

Comforting Bone Broth

Including bone broth in your diet after surgery is an excellent way to meet your hydration needs and improve your healing. It contains an abundance of amino acids, proline and glycine, which assist your body with healing after surgery. Bone broth can be made in big batches and frozen in ice cube trays to drink later. This can also be used as a soup base and can be included in meals throughout your recovery.

Makes: 8 (8-oz [240-ml]) servings

Total Prep Time: 24 hours

Suggested Stages: Pureed, Soft, Regular

2 lb (907 g) chicken bones (may use from a rotisserie chicken)

8 cups (1.9 L) filtered water

2 tbsp (30 ml) apple cider vinegar

2 bay leaves

1 tsp salt, plus more to taste

Place the chicken bones in a large stockpot and cover them with water. Then add the apple cider vinegar, bay leaves and salt and bring everything to a boil over high heat.

Reduce the heat to low. Partially cover the pot and let it simmer for a minimum of 6 hours and up to 24 hours. The longer you let it simmer, the more flavorful and amino-rich it will be.

Remove the broth from the heat and strain it. Season it with extra salt if you desire. Enjoy the broth immediately or store it in Mason jars in the fridge. You may freeze it in ice cube trays if you are not able to use it all within a week.

Notes:

For more flavor, add carrots, onion or celery to the broth while you cook.

Store the broth in the freezer for up to 6 months.

Nutrition Per Serving
Calories: 55, Fat: 2.3, Carbohydrates: <1 g, Fiber: 0 g, Protein: 8.6 g

Peachy Cottage Cheese

A high-protein breakfast is important after surgery, and cottage cheese is a simple ingredient to include to boost your intake. It is a soft protein too, which makes it easier for people to tolerate immediately after surgery. I added canned peaches to this recipe to provide options for those on the soft food diet, but you can change the fruit to fit your needs.

Makes: 4 (¼-cup [60-ml]) servings

Total Prep Time: 15 minutes

Suggested Stages: Soft, Regular

1 cup (240 ml) low-fat cottage cheese

½ cup (124 g) canned peaches, stored in 100% juice, drained

1 tsp cinnamon

Divide the cottage cheese into four separate meal prep containers. Top it with the drained peaches and sprinkle the cinnamon on top. Store this meal in the refrigerator for up to 3 days.

Note: *Once the regular diet stage is reached, nuts can be added.*

Nutrition per serving
Calories: 65, Fat: 2 g, Carbohydrates: 7 g, Fiber: 0 g, Protein: 7 g

Mini Muffin Ham Frittatas

These mini egg bites are inspired by a casserole dish my mother-in-law prepares for holiday mornings. The fire-roasted peppers provide a delicious southwest flavor, but they are not spicy. I love how easy these are to prepare on the weekend and then heat up throughout the week. You can use this recipe as a base and add other non-starchy vegetables if you would like, such as spinach or bell peppers.

Makes: 6 servings (4 egg bites per serving)

Total Prep Time: 30 minutes

Suggested Stages: Soft, Regular

8 eggs

½ tsp salt

⅛ tsp black pepper

¼ cup (60 ml) low-fat milk

2 oz (57 g) ham, sliced into small cubes

4 oz (113 g) canned fire-roasted green peppers

Preheat the oven to 450°F (230°C). Spray a 24-cup mini muffin tin with nonstick cooking spray.

In a medium bowl, whisk together the eggs, salt, pepper and milk. Set aside.

Evenly disperse the ham cubes and fire-roasted peppers into each muffin cup. Then pour the egg mixture into each cup. Bake for 20 minutes, or until the muffins no longer jiggle.

Once cooled, you can either store these in one large meal prep container or in smaller individual containers for a grab-and-go meal. To reheat, place the muffins in the microwave for 30 seconds before eating. You can also store these in the freezer for up to 3 months.

Nutrition Per Serving
Calories: 119, Fat: 7 g, Carbohydrates: 2 g, Fiber: <1 g, Protein: 12 g

Apple Pie Parfait

Including Greek yogurt parfaits in your morning routine will help you meet your protein needs throughout the day. I love the addition of apple spice in this recipe to give it a more familiar flavor, and the pecans provide a crunch, like granola, without the added sugar.

Makes: 2 servings

Total Prep Time: 10 minutes

Suggested Stage: Regular

1 cup (240 ml) plain low-fat Greek yogurt

1 tsp apple spice (see Note)

1 apple (70 g), chopped into small pieces

2 tbsp (15 g) chopped pecans

1–2 tsp (5–10 ml) honey (optional)

Mix the Greek yogurt and apple spice in a small bowl. Divide half of the mixture between two Mason jars.

Next, layer half of the chopped apple between the two jars. Then layer half of the pecans between the jars.

Add the remaining yogurt mixture between the jars. Lastly, layer on the rest of the apples and pecans. Drizzle the honey on top, if desired. Store the parfaits in the refrigerator and remove them when you're ready to eat.

Note: *If you cannot find apple spice, you can substitute with ¾ teaspoon of cinnamon and a pinch of nutmeg.*

Nutrition Per Serving
Calories: 148, Fat: 7.1 g, Carbohydrates: 10.8 g, Fiber: 1.8 g, Protein: 11.8 g

High-Protein Oatmeal Pancakes

This meal is perfect for you if you're looking for a breakfast that has that classic Saturday morning feel. I added vanilla protein powder to increase the protein content in these pancakes. They taste delicious with fresh fruit on the side. I enjoy preparing pancakes in bulk and storing them in the freezer to eat whenever I need them.

Makes: 4 servings (1 pancake per serving)

Total Prep Time: 20 minutes

Suggested Stage: Regular

½ cup (120 ml) low-fat milk

1 cup (80 g) rolled oats

1 egg

1 egg white

½ banana (60 g)

½ scoop (15 g) Isopure vanilla protein powder

2 tbsp (16 g) peanut butter powder

1 tsp vanilla

½ tsp cinnamon

½ cup (83 g) sliced strawberries

Sugar-free syrup (optional)

Blend all of the ingredients, except for the strawberries and syrup, in a blender.

Heat a large nonstick skillet over medium heat and spray it with nonstick cooking oil.

Once heated, pour ⅓ cup (80 ml) of batter onto the skillet. Once bubbles form on the surface, turn the pancake over and cook it for an additional 2 minutes.

Remove it from the heat and repeat for the remaining three pancakes. Divide the pancakes into meal prep containers. If freezing, place them in an airtight container with parchment paper in between each pancake. Another option for meal prep is to only prepare the batter and cook them fresh each day throughout the week. Serve them with fresh strawberries and sugar-free syrup, if desired.

Nutrition Per Serving
Calories: 153, Fat: 2.1 g, Carbohydrates: 20.8 g, Fiber: 3.1 g, Protein: 10.2 g

Ham & Egg Cups

Adding Canadian bacon is an easy way to get protein into your breakfast. It's lower in fat than other breakfast meats like sausage. This recipe keeps it simple with just cheese and an egg added inside, but you could also top it with red pepper or onions for more flavor.

Makes: 3 servings (2 egg cups and 1 mandarin per serving)

Total Prep Time: 20 minutes

Suggested Stage: Regular

6 slices (100 g) Canadian bacon (may use ham slices instead)

⅓ cup (37 g) shredded cheddar cheese

6 eggs

1 tbsp (1 g) chopped cilantro or any other herb of your choice (optional)

3 mandarins (275 g), peeled

Preheat the oven to 400°F (200°C). Spray 6 cups in a 12-cup muffin tin pan with nonstick cooking spray.

Fill the six prepared muffin cups with 1 slice of Canadian bacon to form a small cup. Next, sprinkle the cheddar cheese on top of the ham, evenly between each container. Then crack an egg into each muffin container. It's okay if some of the egg falls below the ham.

Bake them for 12 to 15 minutes. Then remove the cups from the oven and scoop out each muffin with a spoon. Garnish them with cilantro, if desired. To reheat, place them in the microwave for 30 seconds. Serve with some peeled mandarin on the side.

Nutrition Per Serving
Calories: 265, Fat: 16.1 g, Carbohydrates: 12.4 g. Fiber: 1.4 g, Protein: 28.1 g

Breakfast Salad

Salad for breakfast? I know it may sound a little strange, but trust me, it's so good. All the vegetables store well in this salad and it's easy to meal prep ahead of time. I added hard-boiled eggs and breakfast sausage to increase the protein. The lemon and cilantro in this salad really pull the meal together into a delicious combination.

Makes: 3 servings

Total Prep Time: 15 minutes

Suggested Stage: Regular

4 eggs

4 cooked chicken sausage breakfast links (90 g) (I use Aidells Chicken & Apple)

1 cup (165 g) cherry tomatoes, halved

3 tbsp (60 g) chopped red onion

¼ cup (4 g) cilantro, chopped

Juice of 1 lemon

Salt and pepper, to taste

1 avocado (optional)

Add 4 cups (946 ml) of water to a large saucepan and place the eggs in it. Bring the water to a boil and let it boil for 5 minutes.

While the eggs are cooking, cut the chicken sausages into slices and place them in a medium bowl. Then add the tomatoes, red onion and cilantro and mix. Set aside.

Once the eggs are done boiling, remove them from the heat and cool them under cold water. Next, peel and slice the eggs and then add them to the sausage mixture. Add the lemon juice and stir. Add salt and pepper to taste.

Serve the salad immediately or store it in meal prep containers for up to 3 days. Add sliced avocado right before serving, if desired.

Notes:

For a complete meal, add a small piece of fruit.

To boost protein, add two more egg whites.

To keep the avocado fresh once cut, brush the avocado with lemon juice and wrap in plastic wrap.

Nutrition Per Serving (without Avocado)
Calories: 180, Fat: 10.5 g, Carbohydrates: 6.8 g, Fiber: 1 g, Protein: 13 g

Savory Oats

Oatmeal is full of fiber and "good for you" nutrients. But it also lacks protein, which is important after bariatric surgery. I added an egg to help boost the protein content of this recipe. Eggs are full of good nutrients like iron, Vitamin A and choline, so they are a nice combo with the oatmeal.

Makes: 3 servings

Total Prep Time: 15 minutes

Suggested Stage: Regular

¾ cup (60 g) rolled oats

3 eggs

1 turkey bacon strip (11 g), cooked and crumbled

1 green onion (15 g), chopped

Salt and pepper, to taste

Cook the rolled oats according to the package directions.

While the oatmeal is cooking, spray a skillet with cooking spray. Crack the eggs and break them into the skillet. Once the whites begin to set, flip the eggs over and cook the other side until the yolks are cooked to your preference.

Remove the eggs from the skillet. You can prepare the savory oats to eat immediately or divide the food into three different meal prep containers. On top of the oatmeal, add the eggs and garnish with the bacon and green onion. Add salt and pepper to taste. Store them in the refrigerator for up to 3 days. To reheat, cook them in the microwave in 30-second intervals until hot.

Nutrition Per Serving
Calories: 206, Fat: 10.3 g, Carbohydrates: 14.2 g, Fiber: 2.1 g, Protein: 10.6 g

main entrées

The meals on the following pages are designed to be simple and fuel your body after weight-loss surgery. I encourage you to use them as a starting point and tweak them in your own way. If you had surgery less than one year ago, you may need to alter the recipes to meet your smaller portion needs. If you enjoy more spice, feel free to increase the spices. Learning to prepare foods for your body after weight-loss surgery is a process, and I encourage you to be patient and have fun in the kitchen.

poultry

Chicken and turkey may not be easily tolerated in the first few weeks after surgery, but tolerance does improve with time. It's important to make sure you do not overly dry out your poultry, because it becomes harder to swallow. Marinating your meats ahead of time is important, and adding poultry to soups can help improve tolerance.

Chicken Parmesan & Sautéed Zucchini

Chicken Parmesan is one of those dishes that sounds fancy but once you prepare it, you realize how easy it is to put together. I suggest preparing the breaded chicken on your meal prep day and then preparing the rest of the dish on the day you are eating it.

Makes: 4 servings

Total Prep Time: 1 hour

Suggested Stage: Regular

1 egg

1 cup (54 g) whole wheat panko

½ cup (50 g) Parmesan cheese

1 tsp oregano

1 lb (454 g) chicken tenders

2 cups (480 ml) sugar-free marinara sauce

2 oz (57 g) mozzarella, shredded

1 tsp extra virgin olive oil

1½ cups (186 g) chopped zucchini

Salt and pepper

Heat the oven to 450°F (230°C) and line a rimmed baking tray with foil. While the oven is heating, whisk the egg and pour it onto a small plate. In a medium bowl, mix together the panko, Parmesan cheese and oregano. Then pour the mixture onto another small plate.

Dip each chicken tender into the egg and then into the panko mixture. Then place the chicken onto the prepared baking tray. Cook it in the oven for 20 minutes, or until it's cooked all the way through.

While cooking, pour ½ cup (120 ml) of marinara sauce into a small 8 x 8–inch (20 x 20–cm) pan. Then place the chicken on top of the sauce. Layer with the rest of the marinara sauce, then top with the mozzarella. Place the tray back into the oven and cook for an additional 20 minutes. Meanwhile, add the olive oil to a skillet over medium heat. Add the zucchini and sauté for 5 minutes.

To serve, plate the chicken parmesan with the zucchini and add salt and pepper to taste.

Notes: *Use precooked breaded chicken to save time.*

To adapt to the soft diet, sauté the zucchini until soft.

Nutrition Per Serving
Calories: 347, Fat: 12.0 g, Carbohydrates: 31.8 g, Fiber: 4.5 g, Protein: 25.6 g

Quick Honey Chicken Stir-Fry

Including a stir-fry meal during the week is an easy way to use extra veggies you have in the fridge. This recipe uses zucchini and carrots, but you can use whatever veggies you have on hand. Orange juice is used as a natural sweetener in this dish to give it more flavor and reduce the amount of added sugar.

Makes: 4 servings

Total Prep Time: 30 minutes

Suggested Stage: Regular

1 tbsp (15 ml) avocado oil

1 lb (454 g) chicken breast, cut into cubes

1 zucchini (200 g), chopped

1 carrot (50 g), peeled and chopped

⅓ cup (80 ml) reduced-sodium soy sauce

⅓ cup (80 ml) orange juice

⅓ cup (80 ml) + 1 tbsp (15 ml) water, divided

1 tbsp (15 ml) honey (see Notes)

½ tsp minced ginger

1 tbsp (8 g) cornstarch

Heat the oil in a large skillet over medium-high heat. Add the chicken and cook for 7 to 10 minutes, until the chicken is cooked all the way through. Remove the chicken from the skillet and set aside.

In the same skillet, add the chopped veggies and sauté them for 5 to 10 minutes, or until they're lightly browned.

While sautéing the vegetables, in a small bowl, mix together the soy sauce, orange juice, ⅓ cup (80 ml) water, honey and ginger. Once the vegetables are browned, add the mixture to the vegetables and bring it to a boil.

In a small bowl, mix the remaining 1 tablespoon (15 ml) of water and cornstarch. Pour this into the vegetable and soy sauce mixture and continue to boil until the sauce is thickened, 3 to 5 minutes.

Add the chicken back to the skillet with the veggies and sauce. Cook for 1 additional minute. Once finished, eat immediately or place into meal prep containers.

Notes:

Broccoli, cauliflower or snap peas can be substituted for vegetable options.

To make this meal for the whole family, add additional vegetables and serve with a side of brown rice.

Choose a sugar substitute of your choice or omit altogether if you experience dumping with honey.

Nutrition Per Serving
Calories: 208, Fat: 6.7 g, Carbohydrates: 8.1 g, Fiber: 1 g, Protein: 27.6 g

Enchilada-Stuffed Bell Peppers

The enchilada sauce used in this recipe helps keep the meat moist so you will have a higher likelihood of tolerating it. I use ground turkey in this recipe, but you could also use lean ground beef if you prefer. The longer you cook it in the oven, the softer the bell peppers will be.

Makes: 4 servings

Total Prep Time: 30 minutes

Suggested Stage: Regular

1 tbsp (15 ml) olive oil

1 lb (454 g) lean ground turkey

1 onion (140 g), chopped

2 cups (480 ml) enchilada sauce

2 green bell peppers (300 g)

¼ cup (28 g) shredded cheddar cheese

¼ cup (60 ml) low-fat Greek yogurt, for garnish

¼ cup (4 g) cilantro, chopped, for garnish (optional)

Preheat the oven to 400°F (200°C). Line a baking tray with parchment paper or a silicone mat.

In a large skillet, heat the olive oil over medium heat. Add the ground turkey and onion, and sauté until it's cooked all the way through. Use a wooden spoon to break up the meat. Once it's cooked all the way through, add the enchilada sauce. Once everything is done cooking, remove the skillet from the heat.

Slice the stems off the bell peppers, cut them in half lengthwise and remove the seeds. Fill each pepper with the meat mixture. Sprinkle the cheese evenly on top of all the meat-filled bell peppers. Cook for 20 minutes in the oven. Remove them from the oven and serve or store them in meal prep containers. To reheat, place them in the microwave for 45 seconds per bell pepper half. Garnish with Greek yogurt and cilantro before serving.

Note: If you have extra taco meat after filling up each bell pepper, save it for lettuce wraps during the week.

Nutrition Per Serving
Calories: 330, Fat: 16.8 g, Carbohydrates: 18.2 g, Fiber: 4 g, Protein: 27.9 g

Chicken Carrot Pea Mash

You're going to love the simplicity of this meal, and better yet, the flavor. It includes a minimal amount of ingredients that come together very quickly. The peas enhance the flavor of the meal while the chicken is full of protein to help you in your recovery. If you have leftovers, freeze them in ice cube trays to eat another time.

Makes: 4 (¼-cup [60-ml]) servings

Total Prep Time: 15 minutes

Suggested Stages: Pureed, Soft

½ cup (65 g) frozen peas and carrots

4 oz (113 g) rotisserie chicken meat

¼ cup (60 ml) chicken broth, plus more as needed

Add a tablespoon (15 ml) of water to a microwave-safe bowl and then add the frozen pea and carrot mix. Cover and heat in the microwave for 2 minutes. Remove the vegetables and add them to a food processor or blender.

Then add the rotisserie chicken and broth to the blender. Puree until the desired consistency is met. You may need to add additional broth to reach your desired texture.

Portion out the puree into individual meal prep containers. Reheat it in 30-second intervals. If it's too dry when serving, mix in 1 to 2 teaspoons (5 to 10 ml) of chicken broth.

Note: *To include the whole family, serve steamed peas and carrots along with the rotisserie chicken in its whole form.*

Nutrition Per Serving
Calories: 57, Fat: 2 g, Carbohydrates: 1.7 g, Fiber: 0.7 g, Protein: 7.5 g

Tuscan Chicken & White Bean Soup

This soup is simple to make and is packed with nutrients for healing. The cannellini beans provide your body with fiber to promote a healthy digestive tract after surgery. Spinach is added to increase your iron intake and provide color to your meal.

Makes: 6 (½-cup [120-ml]) servings

Total Prep Time: 45 minutes

Suggested Stages: Soft, Regular

1 tbsp (15 ml) extra virgin olive oil

½ onion (125 g), chopped

1 carrot (60 g), chopped

1 zucchini (200 g), chopped

1 celery rib (50 g), chopped (Omit if not recommended by your surgery center)

¼ tsp thyme, dried

½ tsp rosemary, dried

4 cups (960 ml) chicken broth

1 (14-oz [397-g]) can cannellini beans, drained and rinsed

8 oz (226 g) rotisserie chicken, shredded

1 cup (30 g) spinach, chopped

1 tsp salt

½ tsp pepper

1 tbsp (15 ml) white wine vinegar

Add the olive oil to a medium pot. Once heated, add the onion and sauté for 5 minutes. Then add the carrot, zucchini and celery. Sauté for another 5 minutes.

Next, add the thyme, rosemary and chicken broth. Increase the heat to high and bring the soup to a boil. Once boiling, reduce the heat to low and cover. Let simmer for 15 minutes.

Once the vegetables are soft, add the beans and cooked chicken. Simmer for another 3 minutes. Lastly add the spinach, salt, pepper and white wine vinegar. Continue to simmer until the spinach is wilted. Remove from the heat.

Divide the soup between meal prep containers or enjoy it right away. If you have a significant number of leftovers, store them in the freezer for up to 3 months

Notes:

If you cannot tolerate chicken, omit and add another can of cannellini beans.

Serve with toasty bread for the family.

Some surgery centers prohibit the use of celery in the soft diet stage. Please omit if needed.

Nutrition Per Serving
Calories: 182, Fat: 6 g, Carbohydrates: 16 g, Fiber: 5 g, Protein: 15 g

Simple Chicken Salad

After weight-loss surgery, animal proteins may be difficult to tolerate. Canned chicken is a great option after bariatric surgery because it is moist and well-tolerated. Using a light mayo also adds moisture to the dish which may enhance your tolerance. This chicken salad is very basic but as you recover and you can tolerate more foods, you can add your own flavorings such as pecans or grapes.

Makes: 4 (¼-cup [60-ml]) servings

Total Prep Time: 5 Minutes

Suggested Stages: Soft, Regular

1 (12-oz [340-g]) can chicken, drained

3 tbsp (45 ml) reduced-fat mayonnaise or cottage cheese

½ tsp celery seed

¼ tsp onion powder

Salt and pepper, to taste

Mix all of the ingredients together. Divide the chicken salad into meal prep containers then store them in the refrigerator for up to 5 days.

Notes:

If you're in the regular diet stage, you may add pecans or grapes or substitute diced celery for the celery seed and diced onion for the onion powder.

Consider adding ½ to 1 teaspoon of Indian curry powder for a simple variation.

Nutrition Per Serving
Calories: 71, Fat: 4 g, Carbohydrates: 1 g, Fiber: 0 g, Protein: 8 g

Chicken Walnut Mason Jar Salad

Mason jar salads are a great way to incorporate vegetables into your diet. The key with Mason jar salads is to layer the hard vegetables at the bottom with the dressing and to keep the more tender vegetables at the top to prevent the meal from becoming soggy. I recommend using "wide mouth" Mason jars because they are easier to place the vegetables into.

Makes: 4 servings

Total Prep Time: 20 minutes

Suggested Stage: Regular

For the Dressing
3 tbsp (45 ml) balsamic vinegar

¼ cup (60 ml) extra virgin olive oil

1 tsp Dijon mustard

1 tsp honey

⅛ tsp salt

For the Salad
¼ cup (29 g) chopped walnuts

¼ cup (40 g) finely diced red onion

1 celery rib (50 g), diced

1 cup (151 g) red grapes, quartered or halved depending on size

12 oz (340 g) rotisserie chicken meat, shredded

1½ cups (55 g) chopped lettuce or (45 g) spinach if you prefer

In a small bowl, whisk together the ingredients for the salad dressing. Set the mixture aside.

Divide the salad dressing and salad ingredients evenly between the Mason jars in the following order: salad dressing, walnuts, red onion, celery, grapes, shredded chicken and lettuce.

Cover the Mason jars with their lids and store them in the refrigerator until ready to use within 4 days.

Nutrition Per Serving
Calories: 296, Fat: 18.5 g, Carbohydrates: 8.5 g, Fiber: 1.7 g, Protein: 25.8 g

Taco-Stuffed Zucchini Boats

Zucchini boats are an excellent taco shell substitute after weight-loss surgery. They are easy to make, and you can stuff them with any meat or vegetable filling of your choice. This recipe uses a turkey taco meat mixture to provide you with a delicious meal. To help keep the meat mixture moist, the zucchini and taco meat are cooked separately.

Makes: 4 servings

Total Prep Time: 30 minutes

Suggested Stage: Regular

2 medium zucchinis (400 g)

1 tbsp (15 ml) extra virgin olive oil, divided

1 lb (454 g) lean ground turkey

½ cup (80 g) chopped onion

2 tsp (5 g) chili powder

½ tsp cumin

¼ tsp garlic powder

¼ tsp onion powder

½ tsp oregano

½ tsp salt

2 tbsp (32 g) tomato paste

¼ cup (28 g) shredded cheddar cheese

¼ cup (4 g) cilantro

Preheat the oven to 400°F (200°C). Spray a large rimmed baking sheet with nonstick cooking spray or use a silicone mat.

Cut the zucchini in half lengthwise, and scoop out the flesh with a spoon. Brush on 1 teaspoon of olive oil. Then place the zucchini boats on the prepared baking tray and cook them for 15 minutes.

While cooking, heat the remaining 2 teaspoons (10 ml) of olive oil over medium heat in a large skillet. Once hot, add the ground turkey and onion. Brown until the turkey is cooked all the way through, about 8 minutes.

Then add the chili powder, cumin, garlic powder, onion powder, oregano, salt, tomato paste and 2 to 3 tablespoons (30 to 45 ml) of water, depending on how saucy you want the mixture.

Spoon the meat mixture into the zucchini boats then top with the shredded cheese. Place back in the oven for 5 to 10 minutes or until the cheese is melted. Divide them evenly between meal prep containers. Garnish with cilantro before serving.

To reheat, microwave the boats for 90 seconds on high.

Nutrition Per Serving
Calories: 256, Fat: 16.1 g, Carbohydrates: 5 g. Fiber: 1.4 g, Protein: 24.2 g

Chicken Fajita Bowl

Bowls are one of my favorite ways to utilize the Bariatric Plate Method. This one-pan meal makes it super easy to include your protein, vegetable and high-quality carbohydrate in one meal. These chicken fajitas are full of protein and flavor.

Makes: 4 servings

Total Prep Time: 20 minutes

Suggested Stage: Regular

2 tsp (10 ml) olive oil

1 lb (454 g) chicken breast, sliced into strips

1 tsp cumin

1 tsp chili powder

1 tsp salt

½ onion (50 g), sliced

½ red bell pepper (70 g), sliced into strips

1 (15-oz [425-g]) can black beans, drained and rinsed

Juice of 1 lime

½ cup (8 g) cilantro, chopped

Heat the oil in a large skillet and add the chicken breasts. Add the cumin, chili powder and salt. Once cooked through, remove the chicken from the pan.

Then add the onion to the same pan and cook for 5 minutes. Next, sauté the red bell pepper for another 3 minutes. Next, add the black beans. Heat for another 3 minutes. Then add the chicken back in and cook for another minute.

Remove the food from the pan, add the lime juice and garnish with cilantro. Divide equally into meal prep containers, if desired.

Notes:

Use leftover red bell pepper for snacks.

To include the whole family, serve with tortillas.

Nutrition Per Serving
Calories: 276, Fat: 5.9 g, Carbohydrates: 23 g, Fiber: 8.9 g, Protein: 32.7 g

Mason Jar Cobb Salad

Cobb salads are easy to prepare and provide a lot of flavors. The eggs and chicken add a significant amount of protein. I include a homemade dressing in my version to help make it lighter. This salad is stored in a Mason jar to make it an easy grab-and-go meal throughout the week.

Makes: 4 servings

Total Prep Time: 20 minutes

Suggested Stage: Regular

For the Dressing
3 tbsp (45 ml) white wine vinegar

2 tbsp (20 g) minced onion

1 tbsp (15 ml) Dijon mustard

¼ tsp black pepper

¼ tsp salt

3 tbsp (45 ml) olive oil

For the Salad
½ cucumber (80 g), peeled and chopped

1 plum tomato (100 g), chopped

3 slices (51 g) Canadian bacon, chopped

¼ cup (34 g) bleu cheese

8 oz (226 g) rotisserie chicken meat, shredded

2 hard-boiled eggs, sliced in half

1½ cups (55 g) chopped lettuce

In a small bowl, whisk together all the salad dressing ingredients.

Next, layer the following ingredients in order evenly between each of the four Mason jars: salad dressing, cucumber, tomato, bacon, bleu cheese, chicken, egg half and lettuce. Then place on the lids. Store them in the refrigerator for up to 4 days.

Nutrition Per Serving
Calories: 245, Fat: 16.6 g, Carbohydrates: 3.8 g. Fiber: 1.1 g, Protein: 19.2 g

Single-Serving Chicken Pot Pies

If you are looking for that "comfort flavor," look no further than these Single-Serving Chicken Pot Pies. This recipe includes all the flavor of the traditional method but without the extra calories or fat. Wonton wrappers are used as the container. As a bonus, these look so cute in your meal prep containers.

Makes: 6 servings (2 pies per serving)

Total Prep Time: 30 minutes

Suggested Stage: Regular

12 wonton wrappers (3½ x 3½ inches [10 x 10 cm])

¼ cup (57 g) butter

¼ cup (50 g) diced onion

¼ cup (30 g) flour

1 cup (240 ml) chicken broth

¼ cup (60 ml) low-fat milk

8 oz (226 g) rotisserie chicken meat, shredded

1 cup (135 g) frozen peas and carrots

¼ tsp salt

¼ tsp black pepper

Preheat the oven to 375°F (190°C). Spray a 12-cup muffin tin pan with cooking spray. Arrange the wonton wrappers into each cup.

In a large saucepan, melt the butter and sauté the onion for 2 minutes. Then add the flour, broth and milk until the sauce thickens. Next, stir in the cooked chicken, peas and carrots, salt and pepper. Heat everything for 1 minute, then remove the pan from the heat.

Fill each muffin wrapper with ⅓ cup (60 g) of the chicken mixture.

Bake the pot pies for 10 to 15 minutes, then remove them from the oven. Eat them immediately or store them in meal prep containers. To reheat, place the pot pies in the microwave for 30 to 60 seconds.

Note: *If you can't find wonton wrappers, cut egg roll wrappers into 3½-inch (10-cm) squares.*

Nutrition Per Serving
Calories: 217, Fat: 10.9 g, Carbohydrates: 17.5 g, Fiber: 1.4 g, Protein: 12.8 g

Zoodles & Meatballs

This recipe uses a spiralizer, which is a kitchen gadget that makes zucchini into noodles. You can also purchase prepared zucchini noodles to make it faster. You can find these in the produce or freezer section of your grocery store. Zucchini noodles are an excellent pasta substitute if you cannot tolerate pasta, or if you desire a lower carbohydrate option.

Makes: 4 servings

Total Prep Time: 30 minutes

Suggested Stage: Regular

2 medium zucchinis (400 g)

1 (24-oz [680-g]) jar sugar-free marinara sauce

12 oz (340 g) frozen turkey meatballs

1 tsp extra virgin olive oil

Remove the ends from the zucchinis. Cut the zucchinis into noodles in a spiralizer. Set aside.

In a large saucepan, heat the sauce and the meatballs for 20 minutes, or until the meatballs are cooked all the way through.

While the sauce is cooking, add the olive oil to a skillet over medium heat. Once heated, add the zucchini noodles and sauté them for 2 minutes. Do not overcook the zucchini noodles because they will become too soft.

To serve, add the zucchini noodles to the plate and top them with the meatballs and sauce.

Notes:

Add Parmesan cheese for extra flavor.

To spice it up, add crushed red pepper.

To include the whole family, serve with whole-grain pasta noodles.

To adapt for the soft phase, sauté the zucchini for at least 5 minutes or until soft.

Nutrition Per Serving
Calories: 214, Fat: 13.7 g, Carbohydrates: 12.5 g, Fiber: 2.1 g, Protein: 15.7 g

Mason Jar Zucchini Lasagna

Here is an easy Mason jar recipe. Traditionally, lasagna uses ground beef as its protein source, but in this recipe, I chose to use chicken sausage to make it a very easy meal to prepare. I use Aidells Italian chicken sausage, which you can find in most grocery stores. I suggest using 2-cup (480-ml) Mason jars for this recipe because it makes it easier to eat out of the jar without spilling over.

Makes: 4 servings

Total Prep Time: 15 minutes

Suggested Stage: Regular

1 cup (246 g) part-skim ricotta cheese

1 egg

¼ cup (25 g) Parmesan cheese

½ tsp Italian seasoning

½ cup (120 ml) sugar-free marinara sauce

1 medium zucchini (200 g), sliced ¼ inch (6 mm) thick

2 cooked Italian chicken sausages (340 g), sliced

Mix the ricotta, egg, Parmesan cheese and Italian seasoning in a bowl.

Add 1 tablespoon (15 ml) of marinara sauce to the bottom of each jar. Next, layer the sliced zucchini (about three slices), then the chicken sausage (about two to three slices), then 2 tablespoons (31 g) of the ricotta mixture into each jar and cover with 1 tablespoon (15 ml) of marinara. Repeat the layering one more time. Cover the jars with their lids and store them in the refrigerator until ready to use.

When ready, remove the lids and cover the jars with a microwave-safe top, such as a paper towel, and heat for 1 minute. Then remove from the microwave and stir. Cover and return the jar to the micro-wave and heat for another minute, until the internal temperature reaches at least 165°F (75°C).

Notes:

Serve with pasta on the side to enjoy with the family.

If you're able to comfortably eat protein, include 2 to 4 tablespoons (14 to 28 g) of whole-grain pasta on the side.

Nutrition Per Serving
Calories: 222, Fat: 13.5 g, Carbohydrates: 7.1 g, Fiber: 0.7 g, Protein: 18.1 g

Chicken Marsala

Dry chicken can be challenging to tolerate after bariatric surgery. This classic chicken marsala dish has a delicious sauce that adds flavor and moisture to the chicken to make it easier to swallow. I like to pair it with fresh, lightly steamed spinach to make it a more robust meal.

Makes: 4 servings

Total Prep Time: 30 minutes

Suggested Stage: Regular

¼ cup (30 g) flour

¼ tsp salt

⅛ tsp black pepper

1 lb (454 g) chicken breast, thinly sliced

2 tbsp (30 ml) olive oil

½ cup (75 g) chopped onion

1½ cups (105 g) sliced mushrooms

½ cup (120 ml) marsala wine

½ cup (120 ml) chicken broth

2 tbsp (3 g) parsley, chopped, for garnish (optional)

Mix the flour, salt and pepper in a shallow dish. Coat each chicken breast in the mixture and then place them on a clean plate.

Heat the oil in a skillet over medium heat. Add the chicken to the skillet and cook the breasts on each side for 7 to 10 minutes, or until they're completely cooked through. Remove the chicken from the pan.

Next, add the onion and mushrooms to the skillet. Once translucent, about 5 minutes, add the marsala wine and chicken broth and cook for another 2 minutes.

Divide the chicken between meal prep containers and top it with the marsala sauce. Reheat in 30-second intervals in the microwave until the desired temperature is reached. Garnish with the parsley before serving.

Notes:

If you're able to comfortably eat protein, consider pairing this with ¼ cup (28 g) of whole-grain pasta.

To include the whole family, serve with pasta or rice on the side.

If you want to thicken the sauce, you can add 1 teaspoon of cornstarch.

Nutrition Per Serving
Calories: 265, Fat: 10.2 g, Carbohydrates: 9.8 g, Fiber: 0.9 g, Protein: 27.6 g

beef and pork

Beef is high in protein and iron and can add variety to your diet. Don't be alarmed if you cannot tolerate beef in the first 6 months after surgery. It can be helpful to not overcook red meat and use moist cooking methods like the slow cooker, pressure cooker or braising.

Pork adds a lot of flavor to meals and can easily be incorporated into a diet after weight-loss surgery. It's high in protein and includes important nutrients such as thiamine, zinc, iron and vitamin B12.

Grilled Pork Tenderloin with Balsamic Apple Topping

I like to use my barbecue, but grilling your meat may cause the meat to become too tough, so it's important to brush it with olive oil ahead of time. I added the balsamic apple mixture to enhance the sweetness and flavor of the meal.

Makes: 4 servings

Total Prep Time: 30 minutes

Suggested Stage: Regular

2 apples (140 g)

1 tbsp (15 ml) extra virgin olive oil, divided

1 lb (454 g) pork tenderloin, trimmed of fat

¼ tsp salt

½ tsp Italian seasoning

2 tbsp (30 ml) balsamic vinegar

Nutrition Per Serving
Calories: 201, Fat: 6.1 g,
Carbohydrates: 12.6 g,
Fiber: 2.2 g, Protein: 24 g

Preheat the grill to high. While the grill is warming up, cut the apples in half and then brush the flesh of the apples with 1 teaspoon of olive oil.

Brush the pork with the remaining olive oil and sprinkle on the salt. It's important to brush the pork tenderloin with olive oil to help retain its moisture. Grill the pork, turning it occasionally, until the internal temperature is 160°F (70°C), 15 to 18 minutes. While the pork is cooking, add the apples to the grill, flesh side down. Grill them for 4 minutes, then turn them over and cook for an additional 4 minutes. Remove the apples and place them on a cutting board to let them cool. Remove the peel with a fork once cool, then chop the apples and remove the seeds. Set aside.

Next, mix the Italian seasoning and balsamic vinegar. Then add the chopped apples to the mixture. Slice the pork and divide it between meal prep containers. This will store for up to 4 days.

Top the pork with the apple mixture. Reheat it in the microwave in 30-second intervals.

Mini Meatloaf with Broccoli

These mini meatloaves have all the flavor of traditional meatloaf but in a smaller serving. These can easily be made on the weekend, so you have a grab-and-go protein source during the week.

Makes: 12 servings (1 mini meatloaf per serving)

Total Prep Time: 30 minutes

Suggested Stage: Regular

1½ lb (680 g) lean ground beef

1 large egg

¼ cup (60 ml) ketchup

⅓ cup (35 g) breadcrumbs

⅓ cup (30 g) rolled oats

2 tbsp (10 g) celery seed

2 tsp (5 g) onion powder

1 tsp salt, plus more to taste

1 tsp parsley flakes

1½ cups (150 g) chopped broccoli, or any non-starchy vegetable like cauliflower or green beans

Black pepper, to taste

Preheat the oven to 350°F (175°C). Spray a 12-cup muffin tin with nonstick cooking spray. In addition, add 1 inch (2.5 cm) of water to a large saucepan over medium heat.

In a large bowl, mix together all the ingredients, except the broccoli and black pepper, until just combined. Divide the mixture among the 12 muffin tins. Cook them in a preheated oven for 20 to 25 minutes, or until the internal temperature reaches 165°F (74°C).

While the meatloaf is cooking, place the broccoli in a steamer basket, which you'll put inside the saucepan once the water is boiling. Cover the pan with a lid and cook for 5 minutes. Remove it from the heat and season it with salt and pepper to taste.

Once the meatloaves are finished cooking, remove them from the pan and enjoy immediately or store them in meal prep containers, along with the broccoli. If you have leftovers, let them cool and then place them in airtight containers. Freeze leftovers for up to 3 months. Let them thaw in the refrigerator and then reheat them in the microwave until 165°F (74°C), about 2 minutes.

Notes:

You may use large muffin tin containers, but the cooking time will lengthen in the oven.

If you can tolerate larger portions, it's okay to include two muffins per meal.

Nutrition Per Serving

Calories: 128, Fat: 3 g, Carbohydrates: 7.3 g, Fiber: 0.6 g, Protein: 16.6 g

Lemon Herb Pork Chops & Roasted Brussels Sprouts

This is a very easy and delicious way to prepare pork chops. The addition of lemon juice before serving is a must. I included applesauce on the side as a dipping sauce to help sweeten the pork. My whole family loves dipping their pork in applesauce.

Makes: 4 servings

Total Prep Time: 30 minutes

Suggested Stage: Regular

1 egg

½ cup (27 g) whole wheat panko

¼ cup (25 g) Parmesan cheese

1 tsp oregano

1 lb (454 g) thinly sliced pork chops

1½ cups (132 g) Brussels sprouts, cut in half

2 tsp (10 ml) extra virgin olive oil

¼ tsp salt

⅛ tsp black pepper

1 cup (240 ml) no sugar added applesauce

Set the oven to 425°F (218°C) and line a baking tray with a silicone mat or parchment paper.

Whisk the egg and pour it onto a small plate. In a medium bowl, mix together the panko, Parmesan cheese and oregano. Then pour the mixture onto another small plate.

Dip each pork chop into the egg and then dip them into the panko mixture before placing them onto the prepared baking tray.

In a medium bowl, mix together the Brussels sprouts, olive oil, salt and pepper.

Spread the Brussels sprouts around the pork chops. Place the tray in the oven and cook for 20 minutes. Remove the tray and divide the contents into meal prep containers. This will keep for 3 to 4 days.

Serve with applesauce on the side.

Note:

To adapt for the soft stage, I suggest steaming the Brussels sprouts instead.

Nutrition Per Serving
Calories: 321, Fat: 11.6 g, Carbohydrates: 20.1 g, Fiber: 2.7 g, Protein: 33.6 g

Slow Cooker Pulled Pork Bowl

Preparing proteins in the slow cooker after weight-loss surgery is an excellent method to improve tolerance. This recipe uses tenderloin instead of the traditional pork butt to reduce unnecessary fat. If you are cooking for only yourself, I would suggest halving this recipe.

Makes: 4 servings

Total Prep Time: 8 hours

Suggested Stage: Regular

For the Pulled Pork

1 lb (454 g) pork tenderloin, trimmed of fat (see Notes)

2 tbsp (30 ml) extra virgin olive oil

1 cup (240 ml) chicken broth

1 tsp paprika

1 tsp garlic powder

1 tsp mustard powder

1 tsp cumin

Salt and pepper, to taste

For the Coleslaw

1½ cups (105 g) coleslaw mix

⅓ cup (80 ml) reduced-fat mayonnaise

¼ cup (60 ml) white wine vinegar

⅛ tsp salt

2 cups (135 g) frozen corn, defrosted

Place the pork tenderloin in a slow cooker. Pour the olive oil and chicken broth over the tenderloin.

In a small bowl, mix together the paprika, garlic powder, mustard powder and cumin. Sprinkle the mixture over the pork tenderloin until it's well coated. Cook on low for 8 hours. Once it's done, remove the tenderloin from the mixture and shred it with a fork on a plate. Add the shredded pork back to the slow cooker and let it sit in the broth for 5 minutes to absorb the juices.

While the pork is cooking, mix all the ingredients for the coleslaw. Divide the coleslaw mixture between meal prep containers. Top it with the shredded pork and juices when they're done. Place the containers back in the refrigerator and serve the meal cold. The leftovers will store for up to 4 days. Add salt and pepper to taste.

Notes:

You may also use pork butt, but note that it will add additional calories and fat.

You may also use the meat in a pulled pork sandwich if you can tolerate bread.

If you have leftovers, freeze the pulled pork for up to 2 months.

Nutrition Per Serving
Calories: 301, Fat: 13.7 g, Carbohydrates: 18.4 g, Fiber: 2.7 g, Protein: 28.7 g

Mason Jar Hamburger Salad

Burger salads are an easy and healthy way to enjoy some of your favorite foods after weight-loss surgery. This one includes all the yummy toppings like pickles, onions and secret sauce. This recipe uses a Greek yogurt base for the dressing to add a healthy twist to the flavor. Feel free to add whatever toppings you want to make it your own.

Makes: 4 servings

Total Prep Time: 20 minutes

Suggested Stage: Regular

For the Dressing

½ cup (120 ml) low-fat Greek yogurt

2 tbsp (30 g) chopped pickles

2 tsp (10 ml) mustard

2 tbsp (30 ml) ketchup (may use sugar free if desired)

For the Salad

½ tsp avocado oil

1 lb (454 g) lean ground beef

½ onion (125 g), chopped

1 tsp mustard

⅓ cup (53 g) sliced red onion

⅓ cup (50 g) cherry tomatoes, halved

⅓ cup (50 g) dill pickles

1 cup (20 g) lettuce, chopped

In a small bowl, mix together all the ingredients for the dressing. Set the dressing aside.

In a medium skillet, heat the oil. Add the ground beef, breaking it up with a wooden spoon. While browning, add the chopped onion and mustard. Continue to brown the meat until it's cooked all the way through. Remove it from the skillet and allow it to cool.

Divide the dressing into four Mason jars. Next, layer it with the ground beef mixture, red onion, tomatoes, pickles and lettuce. Cover the jars and store them in the fridge for up to 4 days.

Notes:

Add shredded cheddar cheese, if desired.

This also tastes good when it's freshly made while the ground meat is still hot.

Nutrition Per Serving

Calories: 211, Fat: 5.9 g, Carbohydrates: 9.2 g, Fiber: 1.1 g, Protein: 28.7 g

Pineapple Pork Kabobs

It doesn't get much simpler than kabobs. Kabobs are quick to prepare and don't make a big mess in the kitchen. If you have leftovers, you can add the kabob food contents to a salad or a wrap later in the week. This recipe uses pork, but you could easily substitute any protein of your choice. This dish requires marinating to help tenderize the meat.

Makes: 4 servings

Total Prep Time: 1½ hours (includes 1 hour of marinating)

Suggested Stage: Regular

6 oz (180 ml) pineapple juice

⅓ cup (80 ml) reduced-sodium soy sauce

¼ cup (60 ml) honey (see Notes)

2 tbsp (30 ml) extra virgin olive oil

1 lb (454 g) pork tenderloin, cut into 1-inch (2.5-cm) chunks (see Notes)

1 bell pepper (150 g), cut into 1-inch (2.5-cm) slices

1 small pineapple (165 g), cut into cubes

Preheat the grill.

In a medium-size bowl, mix together the pineapple juice, soy sauce, honey and olive oil.

Toss the pork in the sauce and let it marinate for at least 1 hour. Then skewer the pork, bell pepper and pineapple together. Continue to repeat until each skewer is full.

When the grill is ready, heat the skewers on each side for about 4 to 5 minutes.

Notes:

If you are sensitive to honey, substitute with a sweetener of your choice. Since you will not be eating most of the marinade, the amount of sugar your body absorbs will be much less than what is stated in the nutrition facts.

You may substitute with the protein of your choice.

You can serve the meal with white rice to include the whole family.

Nutrition Per Serving
Calories: 394, Fat: 9.7 g, Carbohydrates: 51.8 g, Fiber: 1.8 g, Protein: 26.7 g

seafood

Including seafood in your diet has many benefits. Fatty fish, such as trout and salmon, provide essential omega-3 fatty acids. Your body does not make these fats on its own and it's important you get them from your diet. I also suggest including shrimp in your meal prep because it cooks up fast on a weeknight.

Sheet Pan Pesto Trout with Roasted Tomatoes

Trout is an excellent source of anti-inflammatory fatty acids to help reduce inflammation in your body. I love to use sheet pan meals to prepare my protein and vegetables. Roasted tomatoes have a slightly sweet flavor, and the pesto provides a refreshing complement. Including quinoa as your smart carb will boost your protein and fiber intake.

Makes: 4 servings

Total Prep Time: 30 minutes

Suggested Stage: Regular

½ cup (85 g) quinoa

1 lb (454 g) skin-on trout or salmon

½ cup (120 ml) pesto, divided

2 cups (300 g) grape tomatoes

Preheat the oven to 400°F (200°C). Line a rimmed baking tray with parchment paper or use a silicone mat.

Prepare the quinoa according to the package directions.

Rinse the trout and pat it dry with a paper towel. Place the trout on the baking tray. Spread half of the pesto evenly on top of the trout.

In a bowl, mix together the tomatoes and the remaining pesto. Then place the tomatoes around the trout on the baking tray.

Roast for about 15 minutes, or until the fish can easily flake. Divide the trout, tomatoes and quinoa between meal prep containers. Eat the meal within 2 days and reheat it in 30-second intervals in the microwave.

Nutrition Per Serving
Calories: 356, Fat: 18.3 g, Carbohydrates: 18.4 g, Fiber: 2.9 g, Protein: 28.4 g

Blackened Salmon with Mango Salsa & Roasted Cauliflower

Blackened salmon is one of my favorite ways to eat salmon. The salmon turns black when the spices are heated up to give a more charred look. The mango salsa provides a refreshing taste to this dish and pairs well with the roasted cauliflower. I simply love this dish!

Makes: 4 servings

Total Prep Time: 25 minutes

Suggested Stage: Regular

For the Cauliflower

1½ cups (150 g) cauliflower florets (see Notes)

1 tbsp (15 ml) extra virgin olive oil

¼ tsp salt

For the Mango Salsa

1 cup (165 g) chopped mangos (see Notes)

2 tbsp (20 g) minced onion

1 Roma tomato (60 g), diced

2 tbsp (2 g) cilantro, chopped

Juice of 1 lime

For the Salmon

2 tbsp (30 ml) extra virgin olive oil, divided

1 tsp paprika

½ tsp onion powder

½ tsp garlic powder

½ tsp dried oregano

¼ tsp salt

½ tsp black pepper

12 oz (340 g) salmon, skin removed

Preheat the oven to 375°F (190°C).

Toss the cauliflower florets with olive oil and salt. Arrange the cauliflower on a baking sheet. Roast in the oven for 20 to 25 minutes. Shake the pan at least once to help the cauliflower cook evenly.

While roasting, prepare the mango salsa. Mix the mango, onion, tomato, cilantro and lime juice in a small bowl and set aside.

Heat 1 tablespoon (15 ml) of olive oil in a skillet over medium heat.

To prepare the salmon, in a small bowl, mix the paprika, onion powder, garlic powder, oregano, salt and pepper. Then drizzle 1 tablespoon (15 ml) of olive oil over the salmon. Sprinkle the spice mixture on top of the salmon and press it in with your fingers.

Place the salmon in the skillet and cook it for 3 minutes on each side. Serve it immediately or store it in meal prep containers for up to 3 days. Keep the mango salsa in a separate container, then serve it on top of the salmon when you're ready to eat.

Notes:

To include the whole family, serve this with rice or sweet potatoes on the side.

You may substitute the cauliflower for broccoli or Brussels sprouts.

You may use defrosted frozen mango, if desired.

Nutrition Per Serving

Calories: 221, Fat: 11.4 g, Carbohydrates: 11.5 g, Fiber: 2.4 g, Protein: 20.7 g

Tropical Shrimp Ceviche

When I used to work at a local Mexican restaurant, their tropical ceviche was one of my favorite meals. I really enjoy the sweet and tangy flavors and it's low in fat and processed carbohydrates. It can either be eaten as a snack or a meal. Traditionally, ceviche is paired with tortilla chips, but you can eat it by itself or with a whole grain cracker if you would like.

Makes: 4 (1-cup [240-ml]) servings

Total Prep Time: 30 minutes

Suggested Stage: Regular

Juice of 2 lemons

Juice of 2 limes

12 oz (340 g) cooked shrimp, peeled, deveined and diced (see Notes)

1 cup (165 g) cherry tomatoes, chopped

½ cup (8 g) cilantro

1 mango (150 g), peeled and chopped

¼ cup (40 g) diced red onion

1 avocado (150 g), pitted and diced

In a medium bowl, whisk together the lemon and lime juices. Add the diced cooked shrimp. Marinate for 15 minutes.

Add the rest of the ingredients, except for the avocado, and then divide the ceviche evenly into meal prep containers. When you're ready to eat, add the avocado. This will keep for 3 to 4 days.

Notes:

I use cooked frozen shrimp and then defrost it under cold water before preparing.

To include the whole family, serve with tortilla chips (or corn tortillas for a lower-fat option).

To add extra heat, consider adding chopped jalapeño.

Nutrition Per Serving
Calories: 222, Fat: 6 g, Carbohydrates: 30 g, Fiber: 5 g, Protein: 20 g

Salmon Cake Bento Box

If you need a quick, delicious protein, you'll love these salmon cakes. I use canned salmon since I always have it on hand. You could also use leftover salmon from another meal if you wanted to.

Makes: 3 servings

Total Prep Time: 20 minutes

Suggested Stage: Regular

2 (5-oz [142-g]) cans salmon, drained

1 tsp Old Bay Seasoning

1 egg

1 tbsp (15 ml) low-fat Greek yogurt

½ cup (50 g) whole wheat panko

1 green onion (15 g), minced

½ green bell pepper (75 g), chopped small

1 medium cucumber (50 g), peeled and sliced

½ lemon, sliced, for garnish

Mix the salmon, Old Bay Seasoning, egg, Greek yogurt, panko, green onion and bell pepper together. Form the mixture into six patties.

Heat a skillet over medium heat and spray it with cooking spray. Once heated, add the patties to the skillet. Cook for 3 to 4 minutes on each side. Remove the patties from the skillet.

In meal prep containers, divide the patties and sliced cucumber. Squeeze the lemon juice on before eating.

Note: *This can be adapted to the soft diet by omitting the green onion, bell pepper and cucumber.*

Nutrition Per Serving
Calories: 185, Fat: 4 g, Carbohydrates: 17.9 g, Fiber: 2.3 g, Protein: 19.6 g

Tangy Shrimp Salad with Quinoa

If you are looking for a light lunch for meal prep, you'll love this dish. This recipe is inspired by the popular Vietnamese dish, banh mi. Rice vinegar is used for a tangy taste and the sauce is creamy for a delicious combo. Traditionally this meal is served on a baguette; here I switched it to a lettuce wrap instead so it's not overly filling.

Makes: 4 servings

Total Prep Time: 30 minutes

Suggested Stage: Regular

½ cup (85 g) quinoa

⅓ cup (20 g) chopped cilantro

2 tbsp (30 ml) cottage cheese

2 tbsp (30 ml) low-fat Greek yogurt

2 tbsp (30 ml) lime juice

12 oz (340 g) peeled, deveined, cooked shrimp, tails removed

¼ cup (60 ml) natural rice vinegar

1 small carrot (100 g), peeled and shredded

1 medium cucumber (115 g), sliced and peeled

1 green onion (15 g), sliced

2 cups (40 g) lettuce, chopped

1 avocado (150 g) (optional)

Prepare the quinoa according to the package directions. Once it's finished cooking, allow it to cool.

While the quinoa is cooking, in a medium bowl, combine the cilantro, cottage cheese, yogurt and lime juice. Add in the shrimp and mix.

Layer the following, in order, between four Mason jars: rice vinegar, shrimp mixture, carrot, cucumber, green onion, quinoa and lettuce. It will store for up to 3 days. Slice and serve ¼ of the avocado on top of each jar when serving, if desired.

Note: Quinoa will cool faster if it's placed in a single layer on a plate.

Nutrition Per Serving (without Avocado)
Calories: 192, Fat: 2.3 g, Carbohydrates: 18.2 g, Fiber: 2.6 g, Protein: 25.6 g

vegetarian

Many bariatric post-ops report that vegetarian entrées are easier to tolerate after surgery. If that includes you, then you will enjoy these recipes. They also provide an array of vitamins, minerals and fiber. In the following pages, you will find a variety of options to help support your health goals after weight-loss surgery.

Southwestern Black Bean Burgers

Including black bean patties is a great idea after weight-loss surgery, especially if you are having a challenging time tolerating animal proteins. They keep well in the freezer, and you can add them to salads or lettuce wraps or just have them as a burger if you can tolerate bread.

Makes: 4 servings

Total Prep Time: 30 minutes

Suggested Stages: Soft, Regular

1 (15.5-oz [439-g]) can black beans, drained and rinsed

¼ cup (27 g) breadcrumbs

⅓ cup (70 g) minced bell peppers

¼ cup (35 g) minced onions

1 egg (see Notes)

1 tsp chili powder

1 tsp cumin

3 cloves garlic, minced

Preheat the oven to 375°F (190°C). Line a baking tray with aluminum foil.

In a medium bowl, mash the black beans until they are crumbly. Then add the breadcrumbs, bell pepper, onion, egg, chili powder, cumin and garlic. Mix until everything is evenly distributed. Let the mixture sit for 5 minutes.

Form the mixture into about 5-inch (12.5-cm) patties and place them onto the baking tray. Bake them for 10 minutes on each side. Place them in an airtight container until you're ready to eat. They will stay fresh in the refrigerator for up to 4 days and in the freezer for up to 1 month.

Notes:

You may substitute 1 tablespoon (10 g) of ground flax and 3 tablespoons (45 ml) of water for the egg, if you want to omit it.

This recipe is great for batch cooking to consistently have on hand.

Nutrition Per Serving
Calories: 156, Fat: 2.1 g, Carbohydrates: 25.5 g, Fiber: 8.4 g, Protein: 9.4 g

Single-Serving Ricotta Bake

This recipe might be one of my favorites; it's so easy to make and delicious for the post-op diet phase, plus it's high in protein. This recipe is unique because you prepare it ahead of time and then cook it in the microwave when you're ready to eat it. It is such an easy option. It uses small mason jars, so it stores easily in the refrigerator.

Makes: 4 servings

Total Prep Time: 15 minutes

Suggested Stages: Pureed, Soft, Regular

1 cup (246 g) part-skim ricotta cheese

1 egg

¼ cup (25 g) Parmesan cheese

½ tsp Italian seasoning

½ cup (120 ml) sugar-free marinara sauce, smooth (not chunky), blend beforehand if necessary

Mix the ricotta, egg, Parmesan cheese and Italian seasoning in a bowl.

Add 1 tablespoon (15 ml) of marinara sauce to the bottom of each jar. Then layer one-quarter of the ricotta mixture into each jar. Lastly, top with another layer of sauce (about 1 tablespoon [15 ml]). Cover each jar with a lid and store them in the refrigerator until ready to use. This will stay fresh for 3 to 4 days.

When ready, remove the lid from the jars and cover them with a microwave-safe top, such as a paper towel, and heat for 1 minute in the microwave. Then remove and stir. Return the jar to the microwave and heat for another minute until the internal temperature reaches at least 165°F (74°C). Enjoy!

Notes:

Serve with pasta on the side to enjoy with the family.

If you're past the pureed diet phase, there is no need to blend the marinara sauce beforehand.

Nutrition Per Serving
Calories: 124, Fat: 7.5 g, Carbohydrates: 3.4 g, Fiber: 0 g, Protein: 10.5 g

Quick Indian Lentil Soup

If you're looking for something quick and easy to make, then this Indian lentil soup is perfect. To help reduce time in the kitchen, I use canned lentils. Then you just add your spices and broth and cook accordingly. Lentils contain protein and fiber to help with your digestion after surgery.

Makes: 2 (1-cup [240-ml]) servings

Total Prep Time: 15 minutes

Suggested Stages: Soft, Regular

1 tsp olive oil

½ onion (80 g), diced

1 tbsp (5 g) Indian curry powder

1 (15-oz [425-g]) can lentils, rinsed and drained

1½ cups (360 ml) chicken broth

Salt and pepper, to taste

Heat the oil in a saucepan over medium heat. Add the diced onion and sauté for 3 minutes. Add the curry powder and sauté for another minute or so.

Then add the lentils and broth. Bring everything to a simmer. Cover the saucepan and cook for another 10 minutes.

Divide the soup into meal prep containers. To reheat, microwave it in 30-second intervals until reaching your desired temperature. Add salt and pepper to taste. This will keep for 3 to 4 days.

Notes: *To serve with family, double the recipe and add crusty bread or naan on the side.*

To adapt for the puree phase, place in blender and puree until smooth.

Nutrition Per Serving
Calories: 222, Fat: 3 g, Carbohydrates: 32 g, Fiber: 7 g, Protein: 15 g

High-Protein Carrot Ginger Soup

Right after surgery, you may feel nauseous. While it's important to communicate your symptoms with your doctor, you may be able to alleviate the nausea with ginger. This soup incorporates ginger, which may help relieve your discomfort. I also added unflavored protein powder to it to increase the protein. The key to adding protein powder is not to add it until the dish is below 140°F (60°C). You may also continue to include this soup in your diet during the soft food or regular diet phase.

Makes: 5 (½-cup [120-ml]) servings

Total Prep Time: 30 minutes

Suggested Stages: Pureed, Soft, Regular

1 tbsp (15 ml) extra virgin olive oil

½ onion (70 g), chopped

8 oz (226 g) baby carrots

½ tsp salt

1 tbsp (1 g) minced ginger

2 cups (480 ml) chicken broth

2 scoops (60 g) unflavored protein powder (I use Isopure)

1 tsp dried parsley, for garnish (optional)

Heat the olive oil over medium heat in a saucepan. Add the onion and carrots and sauté for 5 to 8 minutes, or until the onion is translucent. Then add the salt, ginger and broth. Bring it to a boil, then lower the heat and simmer, covered, for 20 minutes.

Once the carrots are soft, add the soup to the blender and puree until the consistency is smooth.

Once the temperature drops below 140°F (60°C), add the unflavored protein powder. If it is added before this, it will become clumpy.

Divide the soup into meal prep containers and garnish with dried parsley, if desired. This will keep for 4 to 5 days.

Notes:

You may freeze leftovers for up to 3 months. I suggest freezing them in silicone ice cube trays for smaller portion sizes.

Once you're in the regular diet stage, you may substitute green onions for the dried parsley.

Nutrition Per Serving
Calories: 90, Fat: 2.9 g, Carbohydrates: 6.1 g, Fiber: 1.6 g, Protein: 10.6 g

Black Bean Dip

Plant-based proteins, such as beans, are well tolerated after bariatric surgery. This bean dip tastes delicious as a meal or snack. You may notice it has a higher carbohydrate amount than other early post-op food choices, which may make you feel uncomfortable. Since it's a high fiber carbohydrate choice, it will not derail your weight loss efforts. This dip is great served as is during the early stages after post-op but can also be used as a dip when your diet advances to regular.

Makes: 4 (¼-cup [60-ml]) servings

Total Prep Time: 5 minutes

Suggested Stages: Pureed, Soft, Regular

1 (15-oz [425-g]) can black beans, drained and rinsed

½ cup (120 ml) low-fat Greek yogurt

½ tsp cumin

¼ tsp chili powder

Juice of 1 lime

Place all the ingredients in a food processor or blender and puree until the desired texture is achieved.

Divide the dip into individual meal prep containers. This will keep for 3 to 4 days.

Notes:

You may add unflavored protein powder to boost protein.

Serve with carrots or celery sticks if you've advanced to the regular diet stage.

Nutrition Per Serving
Calories: 136, Fat: 1 g, Carbohydrates: 24.1 g, Fiber: 7.7 g, Protein 9.8 g

Egg Drop Soup

This egg drop soup is a flavorful and delicious way to add protein into your diet after surgery. I used to believe egg drop soup would be challenging to prepare but it is surprisingly easy. I use frozen peas and carrots to make prep time as simple as possible. During the early stages after surgery, it may take you 30 to 60 minutes to consume this meal. It's okay to just sip on it.

Makes: 4 (1-cup [240-ml]) servings

Total Prep Time: 15 minutes

Suggested Stages: Soft, Regular

4 cups (960 ml) chicken broth (see Notes)

1 tsp garlic powder

½ tsp ground ginger

1 tsp onion powder

4 eggs

1 cup (135 g) frozen peas and carrots

¼ tsp toasted sesame oil

Reduced-sodium soy sauce (optional)

Add the chicken broth, garlic powder, ground ginger and onion powder to a saucepan and heat over medium heat. Bring it to a simmer.

Meanwhile, whisk together the eggs in a liquid measuring cup. Once the mixture is simmering, slowly pour the egg mixture into the broth while whisking the broth. Once all the eggs are completely mixed, add the frozen peas and carrots. Bring it back to a simmer and cook for an additional 8 minutes.

Divide the soup evenly between meal prep containers or serve immediately. This will keep for 3 to 4 days.

Notes:

Use bone broth instead of chicken broth to add extra protein.

Once you're in the regular diet stage, you can add green onion as a garnish.

Nutrition Per Serving
Calories: 113, Fat: 6.5 g, Carbohydrates: 5.3 g, Fiber: 1 g, Protein: 8.3 g

Falafel Lettuce Wraps with Hummus

Chickpeas are so versatile and are used in this recipe as a plant-based protein. Falafel is made from chickpeas and is very flavorful. In this recipe, I stuff them in a lettuce wrap. You could also add falafel to salads or enjoy in a small pita if desired. Falafel freezes well and can be stored in the freezer for up to 2 months and is a great option for meal prepping.

Makes: 4 servings (1 lettuce leaf, 2 falafel and 2 tbsp [30 ml] hummus per serving)

Total Prep Time: 40 minutes

Suggested Stage: Regular

1 (15-oz [425-g]) can chickpeas, drained, rinsed and patted dry

½ cup (30 g) chopped parsley

⅓ cup (53 g) chopped onion

4 cloves garlic, minced

2 tbsp (18 g) raw cashews

1 tsp cumin

¼ tsp cardamom

¼ tsp salt

¼ tsp black pepper

4 lettuce leaves

½ cup (120 ml) hummus

To meal prep, make the chickpea mixture on meal prep day and cook it on the day you want to eat it. In a blender or food processor, pulse the chickpeas, parsley, onion, garlic, cashews, cumin, cardamom, salt and pepper until it's crumbly. Then form the mixture into 2-inch (5-cm) balls and place them on a baking sheet.

When you're ready to eat, preheat the oven to 425°F (220°C) and spray a baking sheet with cooking spray or line it with a silicone mat.

Place it in the oven and bake the falafel for 25 minutes, flipping once halfway through. Remove the tray from the oven. When storing, keep the lettuce separate from the chickpeas and assemble when eating.

When serving, place two falafel in a lettuce wrap and top with hummus.

Nutrition Per Serving
Calories: 198, Fat: 7.1 g, Carbohydrates: 26.9 g, Fiber: 7.4 g, Protein: 8.8 g

Cashew Tofu

Tofu is an excellent high-protein option when you don't feel like eating meat or desire more of a plant-based lifestyle. It's not as protein-dense as animal products but works well in most dishes as a plant-based substitute because it takes on the flavor of the sauces. This recipe uses hoisin sauce, which can be found in the Asian food section of your local grocery store.

Makes: 3 servings

Total Prep Time: 20 minutes

Suggested Stage: Regular

For the Tofu

1 tbsp (15 ml) reduced-sodium soy sauce

2 tsp (5 g) cornstarch

12 oz (340 g) extra-firm tofu

2 tbsp (30 ml) avocado oil

1 tbsp (15 g) minced garlic

1 tbsp (6 g) grated ginger

1 red bell pepper (110 g), chopped

½ onion (80 g), chopped

¼ cup (36 g) unsalted cashews

¼ cup (4 g) cilantro, for garnish (optional)

For the Sauce

2 tbsp (30 ml) hoisin sauce

1 tbsp (15 ml) reduced-sodium soy sauce

1 tbsp (15 ml) rice vinegar

1 tbsp (8 g) cornstarch

¼ cup (60 ml) water

In a medium bowl, mix together 1 tablespoon (15 ml) of soy sauce and the cornstarch. Set aside. In another small bowl, mix together all the ingredients for the sauce. Set aside.

Remove the tofu from the packaging and dry it with a paper towel. Then cut the tofu into 1-inch (2.5-cm) cubes. Add the tofu to the soy sauce and cornstarch mixture. Toss to coat it and set aside.

In a skillet over medium heat, warm the avocado oil. Once it's hot, add the garlic and ginger and sauté for 1 minute. Then add the tofu mixture. Cook for 7 minutes. Then add the red bell pepper and onion. Sauté for another 3 minutes, then add the sauce and cashews. Continue to sauté until everything is heated through, about 2 minutes.

Divide evenly into meal prep containers and sprinkle with cilantro, if desired. This will keep for 3 to 4 days.

Notes:

To include the whole family, serve over long-grain brown rice.

To sweeten, you can add 1 teaspoon of honey.

Nutrition Per Serving
Calories: 315, Fat: 20.6 g, Carbohydrates: 17.2 g, Fiber: 2.9 g, Protein: 16.6 g

snacks

Snacks can be included as a tool to help you meet your daily protein goals. Ideally, you want to include more whole food snacks in your routine instead of processed snacks to prevent becoming overly hungry during the day. They are also a good opportunity to include more vegetables and fruits in your diet. The snacks on the following pages are designed to not only provide you with energy, but also to nourish your body.

Red Pepper Hummus with Baby Carrots

Store-bought hummus can be high in fat and low in protein for the bariatric post-op. Preparing your own at home lets you be in charge of the ingredients, and you can lower the fat intake. You can add whatever flavors you want to make it your own. In this dish, I chose to add roasted red pepper to boost the nutrients and flavor.

Makes: 4 servings

Total Prep Time: 10 minutes

Suggested Stage: Regular

1 (15-oz [425-g]) can chickpeas, drained and rinsed

2 cloves garlic

2 tsp (4 g) ground cumin

¼ tsp salt

½ cup (130 g) roasted red bell peppers (see Notes)

1–2 tbsp (15–30 ml) water or vegetable broth

1½ cups (165 g) baby carrots or any other raw vegetable of choice

In a food processor, blend all of the ingredients except for the water and carrots. A thick paste should form. Then add the water or broth, 1 tablespoon (15 ml) at a time, until the desired thickness is achieved. Serve with baby carrots.

Notes:

Substitute the red bell pepper for basil if desired.

Add unflavored protein powder for an extra protein boost.

May be adapted for the pureed and soft stage by omitting the baby carrots.

Nutrition Per Serving
Calories: 124, Fat: 2.5 g, Carbohydrates: 20.3 g, Fiber: 6.5 g, Protein: 6.2 g

Zucchini Pizza Bites

These zucchini pizza bites are fast and, best of all, very satisfying. I like to serve these as an appetizer if I'm entertaining or for a quick snack in the afternoon. They taste just like pizza, but they are more in alignment with your health goals. I suggest using a mandolin if you have one to slice the zucchini, but you can also slice by hand.

Makes: 4 servings

Total Prep Time: 15 minutes

Suggested Stage: Regular

1 medium zucchini (200 g), sliced

½ cup (120 ml) sugar-free marinara sauce

½ cup (50 g) shredded mozzarella

½ tsp Italian seasoning

Preheat the oven to 450°F (232°C). Line a baking sheet with parchment paper or a silicone mat.

Slice the zucchini into ¼-inch (6-mm) slices, which provides about 24 slices. Then place them on the prepared baking sheet.

Evenly distribute the marinara sauce and mozzarella on top of each zucchini slice, and then sprinkle on the Italian seasoning.

Cook for 5 minutes, or until the cheese becomes bubbly. To meal prep, slice the zucchini ahead of time and make them as you go.

Nutrition Per Serving

Calories: 50, Fat: 2.7 g, Carbohydrates: 3.5 g, Fiber: 0.7 g, Protein: 3.1 g

Smoked Salmon Snack Box

Bento boxes are one of my favorite meal prep meals. You can create different combinations depending on what you have on hand in your house. This bento box includes smoked salmon, which has a lot of flavor and contains omega-3 fatty acids. The cucumber has a nice refreshing flavor, and it reminds me of a sushi concoction when combined with rice vinegar.

Makes: 4 servings

Total Prep Time: 15 minutes

Suggested Stage: Regular

9 oz (255 g) smoked salmon

1 medium cucumber (300 g), peeled and sliced

¼ cup (60 ml) rice vinegar (without added sugar)

4 small mandarins (300 g), peeled

Evenly divide the ingredients between the meal prep containers. You can store them in the refrigerator for up to 3 days.

Nutrition Per Serving
Calories: 119, Fat: 3 g, Carbohydrates: 11.1 g, Fiber: 1.5 g, Protein: 12.4 g

Easy Parmesan Crisps

When you're in the soft diet phase, sometimes you crave something "crunchy." This recipe will do just the trick. These one-ingredient crisps are quick to prepare and will become one of your favorite snacks.

Makes: 8 servings (2 crisps per serving)

Total Prep Time: 15 minutes

Suggested Stages: Soft, Regular

¾ cup (75 g) shredded Parmesan cheese

Preheat the oven to 400°F (200°C).

Line a rimmed baking sheet with parchment paper or a silicone mat. Spread a single layer of Parmesan cheese across the entire baking sheet.

Bake for 3 to 6 minutes. Remove the tray from the oven and let the cheese cool completely. Once cool, break the baked cheese into 16 separate squares and store them in an airtight container in the refrigerator for 4 to 5 days.

Note: *Store them in separate baggies for portion control.*

Nutrition Per Serving
Calories: 39, Fat: 3 g, Carbohydrates: 0 g, Fiber: 0 g, Protein: 3 g

Watermelon Mint Popsicles

During the pureed and soft food diet phases, you may be craving something with a little "texture." Including sugar-free popsicles is an excellent way to meet your hydration needs while also satisfying your desire for more "texture" if you crunch it. I included watermelon and mint in these popsicles, but you can easily include whatever fruit or herbs you enjoy.

Makes: 8 servings

Total Prep Time: 5 hours

Suggested Stages: Pureed, Soft, Regular

4 cups (960 ml) water

6 mint sprigs (3 g), washed

1 cup (140 g) cubed watermelon

1–2 drops stevia (optional)

Fill a large pitcher with the water and add the mint and watermelon. Cover it with a lid and store it in the fridge for at least 1 hour.

Strain the water and then pour it into the popsicle molds. Store them in the freezer for at least 4 hours before eating.

Notes:

If you don't have popsicle molds, you can add the liquid to ice cube molds.

If you want flavored water, you could also use half of this recipe for an infused water beverage and half for popsicles.

Nutrition Per Serving
Calories: 0, Fat: 0 g, Carbohydrate: <1 g, Dietary Fiber: 0 g, Protein: 0 g

Blueberry Coconut Trail Mix

Store-bought trail mix can be high in sugar and fats. This homemade version includes whole, fresh blueberries which will keep you more satisfied than dried fruit and prevent blood sugar spikes. Shredded coconut provides a tropical sweet flavor to the mix. I like to pack mine in single-serving baggies and store them in the refrigerator to eat when hunger strikes.

Makes: 4 servings

Total Prep Time: 10 minutes

Suggested Stage: Regular

2 cups (296 g) blueberries or strawberries

½ cup (47 g) unsweetened shredded coconut

½ cup (54 g) raw cashews, walnuts or almonds

Mix all of the ingredients together in a small bowl. Evenly divide the mix between meal prep containers.

Cover and store the containers in the refrigerator until you're ready to eat.

Nutrition Per Serving
Calories: 204, Fat: 13.3 g, Carbohydrates: 20.1 g, Fiber: 4.5 g, Protein: 4.7 g

Frozen Mini Chocolate Peanut Butter Cups

One of the best combinations is chocolate and peanut butter (in my humble opinion). This peanut butter cup recipe can be made ahead of time and stored in the freezer for whenever you have a little sweet tooth. It uses peanut butter powder to reduce unnecessary calories while also providing lots of flavor (and protein too). It's seriously so good!

Makes: 8 servings (3 pieces per serving)

Total Prep Time: 70 minutes (includes freezing time)

Suggested Stage: Regular

8 oz (226 g) sugar-free chocolate chips

¼ cup (32 g) peanut butter powder (I use PB2)

¼ cup (60 ml) water

In a small bowl, add the chocolate chips. Place the bowl in the microwave and heat the chocolate chips for 20 seconds. Remove and stir. Place the bowl back in the microwave for another 20 seconds. Stir and continue the process until the chips are melted.

Line each cup in a 24-cup mini muffin tin with a muffin liner. Then add a teaspoon of the melted chocolate onto the bottom of each muffin tin container.

Next, mix together the peanut butter powder and water. Once it reaches a thick consistency, layer the mixture on top of the first chocolate layer in the muffin tins. Then layer the remaining chocolate mixture evenly on top of the peanut butter mixture.

Place the muffin tin in the freezer for at least 30 minutes. Continue to store them in the freezer until you're ready to eat the peanut butter cups.

Note: *If you're struggling with portion control, it may be best to store these each in individual baggies.*

Nutrition Per Serving
Calories: 118, Fat: 9 g, Carbohydrates: 17 g, Fiber: 11 g, Protein: 4 g

Raspberry Dark Chocolate Chia Seed Pudding

Have I mentioned I love chocolate? This simple chia seed pudding is very chocolatey and is the perfect snack when you are looking for something sweet. It has a ton of fiber to help with your digestion which is a bonus.

Makes: 2 (½-cup [120-ml]) servings

Total Prep Time: 3 hours (includes chill time)

Suggested Stage: Regular

¾ cup (180 ml) low-fat milk

3 tbsp (30 g) chia seeds

3 tbsp (20 g) cocoa powder

1 tbsp (16 g) almond butter

2 tsp (10 ml) sugar-free maple syrup

⅓ tsp vanilla extract

¼ tsp salt

½ cup (62 g) raspberries

Add all the ingredients, except for the raspberries, into a blender and blend for 2 to 3 minutes, until thickened, smooth and creamy.

Divide the mixture into meal prep containers and store them in the fridge for at least 3 hours and up to 3 days. Top with raspberries when you're ready to eat.

Nutrition Per Serving
Calories: 231, Fat: 12.6 g, Carbohydrates: 26.1 g, Fiber: 11.9 g, Protein: 9.8 g

Lime Chia Seed Pudding

The taste of lime reminds me of summer and freshness. This lime chia seed pudding has a refreshing flavor and is a light snack. The chia seeds provide extra fiber and nutrients to your diet. This is a delicious treat the whole family will enjoy.

Makes: 2 (½-cup [120-ml]) servings

Total Prep Time: 2 hours

Suggested Stage: Regular

3 tbsp (30 g) chia seeds

Juice of 1 lime

½ cup (120 ml) low-fat Greek yogurt

½ cup (120 ml) almond milk

1 tsp sugar-free maple syrup or substitute sweetener of your choice

Optional Toppings
Shredded coconut, graham crackers or matcha green tea powder to make green (contains caffeine)

Mix all of the ingredients in a bowl and then divide the mixture evenly between meal prep containers. Store for at least 2 hours and up to 3 days.

Notes: *Some surgery centers allow chia seeds in the soft diet stage. Check your surgery center's guidelines to see if these would be allowed.*

The picture includes matcha green tea powder for color.

Nutrition Per Serving
Calories: 186, Fat: 10 g, Carbohydrates: 15 g, Fiber: 7 g, Protein: 10 g

Caprese Salad

My family is Italian and I always loved when my mom served me caprese salad with fresh tomatoes and basil from the garden during the summer. As I've gotten older, I've begun adding red onion for a delicious flavor combination. It also serves as a high-protein snack after weight-loss surgery.

Makes: 4 servings

Total Prep Time: 10 minutes

Suggested Stage: Regular

8 oz (226 g) mozzarella balls (stored in water)

6 basil leaves (6 g), chopped

1 cup (165 g) cherry tomatoes

¼ cup (20 g) chopped red onions

2 tsp (10 ml) extra virgin olive oil

2 tsp (10 ml) balsamic vinegar

Salt and pepper, to taste

Combine the mozzarella balls, basil, cherry tomatoes and red onion in a small bowl. Drizzle the olive oil and balsamic vinegar on top. Then divide the salad between meal prep containers. Store it in the refrigerator for up to 3 days.

Nutrition Per Serving
Calories: 176, Fat: 11.5 g, Carbohydrates: 4.2 g, Fiber: 0.6 g, Protein: 14.2 g

Carrot Spice Mini Muffins

Little muffins are so fun to make and can help provide you with a portion control snack. As an extra bonus, kids in the household usually enjoy eating them too. This recipe calls for maple syrup for a little bit of sweetness. Even though it's a small amount, if this bothers your tummy, then you can use 1 to 2 drops of stevia for this meal.

Makes: 6 servings (4 muffins per serving)

Total Prep Time: 45 minutes

Suggested Stage: Regular

1 cup (95 g) almond flour

¼ cup (32 g) coconut flour

1 tsp baking soda

½ tsp salt

1 tsp cinnamon

1 tbsp (10 g) chia seeds

1 banana (130 g)

1 tbsp (15 ml) extra virgin olive oil

3 eggs

2 tbsp (30 ml) maple syrup

2 carrots (120 g), grated

Preheat the oven to 350°F (175°C). Spray a 24-cup mini muffin tin with cooking spray.

In a medium bowl, mix together the almond flour, coconut flour, baking soda, salt, cinnamon and chia seeds.

In a large bowl, mash the banana. Once it's mashed, add the olive oil, eggs and maple syrup. Once everything is thoroughly mixed together, add the dry ingredients until it's all combined. Stir in the grated carrots.

Ladle the mixture into each muffin cup (about 2 tablespoons [30 ml] each). Bake them for 30 minutes. Store the muffins in an airtight container in the fridge for up to 4 days.

Nutrition Per Serving
Calories: 211, Fat: 9.3 g, Carbohydrates: 12.3 g, Fiber: 3.8 g, Protein: 7.4 g

Sweet Balsamic Strawberries & Mint

This recipe is a unique combination, but it has a yummy flavor. The strawberries and mint offer a refreshing taste, while the balsamic dressing adds a sweet and savory flavor. The ricotta is very mellow and balances the dish while adding a protein boost.

Makes: 4 servings

Total Prep Time: 10 minutes

Suggested Stage: Regular

1 cup (246 g) part-skim ricotta cheese

1 tbsp (1 g) mint, chopped

1 cup (166 g) sliced strawberries

1 tsp balsamic vinegar

Honey (optional)

In separate meal prep containers, evenly divide the ricotta cheese. Then top each container with the mint and strawberries. Store them in the refrigerator for up to 3 days. At the time of serving, drizzle ¼ teaspoon of balsamic vinegar and honey, if desired, over the top.

Note: Use leftover mint for a refreshing mint-infused water.

Nutrition Per Serving (without Honey)
Calories: 104, Fat: 5 g, Carbohydrates: 7.6 g, Fiber: 0.8 g, Protein: 7.43 g

Parmesan-Roasted Edamame

I love this for a quick and easy high-protein snack. Edamame is high in protein and develops a delicious nutty flavor when roasted in the oven. This recipe adds Parmesan cheese, but you can add whatever seasonings you desire.

Makes: 4 servings

Total Prep Time: 20 minutes

Suggested Stage: Regular

2 tsp (10 ml) extra virgin olive oil

1 (10-oz [283-g]) package frozen shelled edamame

½ cup (50 g) grated Parmesan cheese

Cayenne pepper (optional)

Heat the oven to 375°F (190°C).

In a medium bowl, toss together the olive oil and edamame. Arrange the edamame in a single layer on a baking sheet. Roast them for 12 to 15 minutes. When you remove the baking sheet, sprinkle the edamame with Parmesan cheese and cayenne pepper, if desired. Enjoy them immediately or store them in separate airtight containers to enjoy throughout the week.

Note: *The edamame pairs well with grapes if you want to add extra carbs.*

Nutrition Per Serving
Calories: 179, Fat: 10.2 g, Carbohydrates: 8.6 g, Fiber: 5.2 g, Protein: 15.9 g

High-Protein Berry Popsicles

Sometimes I'm in the mood for a cold treat and these yummy popsicles are perfect. I use Greek yogurt and add vanilla protein powder for a protein boost. I love that these can be adapted with any frozen fruit you have on hand or used with any of your preferred protein powders.

Makes: 4 servings (1 popsicle per serving)

Total Prep Time: 4 hours and 10 minutes

Suggested Stage: Regular

1 cup (240 ml) low-fat Greek yogurt

1 cup (150 g) frozen berries (see Note)

1 tsp maple syrup

1 tsp vanilla extract

1 scoop (30 g) vanilla protein powder

Stir all of the ingredients together. Then place the mixture into popsicle molds and stick popsicle sticks halfway in. Place them in the freezer for at least 4 hours.

Note: *Have fun with this recipe and swap out the berries for your favorite fruit.*

Nutrition Per Serving
Calories: 89, Fat: 1.2 g, Carbohydrates: 7.9 g, Fiber: 1 g, Protein: 11.4 g

Apple & Peanut Butter Dip

Sometimes you want something sweet. This is the perfect dish for that moment. It's not only sweet but it also has protein and fiber. This stores well in a divided meal prep container, and you can pop it out whenever you have a sweet tooth.

Makes: 2 servings

Total Prep Time: 10 minutes

Suggested Stage: Regular

⅔ cup (160 ml) low-fat vanilla Greek yogurt

¼ cup (32 g) peanut butter powder

1 apple (150 g), sliced (see Note)

Mix the yogurt and peanut butter powder together. Store the mixture in a meal prep container.

Serve with the sliced apple.

Note: *You may substitute the fruit for your personal preference.*

Nutrition Per Serving
Calories: 200, Fat: 6, Carbohydrates: 21 g, Fiber: 5 g, Protein: 16 g

Edamame Bento Box

These quick and easy snack boxes are so helpful to have on hand. I use frozen, shelled edamame and then defrost them under water before placing them in the snack boxes. Feel free to mix and match the fruit and vegetables to your personal preference.

Makes: 2 servings

Total Prep Time: 10 minutes

Suggested Stage: Regular

1½ cups (150 g) edamame, shelled

1½ cups (150 g) grapes

1 cup (150 g) baby carrots

Salt and pepper, to taste (optional)

Evenly divide the shelled edamame, grapes and carrots between the snack boxes. Add salt and pepper to the edamame, if desired, before eating.

Note: *Drizzle rice vinegar on top of the edamame before eating for extra flavor.*

Nutrition Per Serving
Calories: 201, Fat: 4.5 g, Carbohydrates: 33.4 g, Fiber: 7.4 g, Protein: 11.2 g

acknowledgments

This cookbook would not be possible without the efforts of many. First and foremost, thank you to my husband, who believes in me, supports me and provides me the space to create new recipes for my loyal weight-loss surgery community. And thank you to my wonderful kids, Emma and Jacob, for taste testing and being a part of this process, whether you knew it or not.

I'm grateful to Page Street Publishing and my editor, Tamara Grasty, for providing me the opportunity to deliver this resource to the bariatric community.

And lastly, thank you to my parents for always supporting my goals and nurturing my curiosity.

about the author

Kristin Willard is a registered dietitian who specializes in bariatric nutrition. She teaches bariatric pre- and post-op clients how to eat healthily and keep their weight off after surgery.

Kristin has been a registered dietitian for ten years and was frustrated with the lack of nutrition resources for her bariatric clients. She created BariatricMealPrep.com to deliver recipes, meal prep ideas, credible nutrition advice and inspiration for those considering or those who have undergone weight-loss surgery. She is an integrative member of the American Society of Metabolic and Bariatric Surgery (ASMBS) and delivers online nutrition programs to those who have had weight-loss surgery.

index